"In this fine work, Prof. Smudde fill
dialogue surrounding the integrat
reer path. *Faithful Careers* will serve as a powerful discernment tool to
help anyone interested in the Catholic faith to first become well informed
about the rich spirituality and theology of human labor and then to apply
that experience in making wise and holy career choices. The practical
points for prayer and suggested plans for action that are included with
each chapter will systematically direct readers along a vocational journey that renders daily life more meaningful as the workplace becomes
more faith full."

— *Fr. John Kartje, Rector, Mundelein Seminary*

"In *Faithful Careers* Pete Smudde shares his Catholic journey in a poignant and thoughtful narrative. He clearly lays out a foundational truth
about the Catholic faith: to be a faithful worker is to work at one's own
faith. In sharing his own reflections on the integration of work and faith,
Smudde encourages every Catholic to find their faith in their work and
to see it not simply as a job, but as a vocation we are called to by God.
He carefully and cogently wields scripture and Catholic teachings not for
a theological argument, but for an exercise in deep personal introspec-
tion. This is a must-read for any Catholic, and any person seeking to find
meaning in their daily efforts."

— *Joseph M. Valenzano III, Ph.D., Professor,*
University of Dayton

"Dr. Smudde has shown a spotlight on the importance of understanding
God's will from a holistic vantage point and integrating that knowledge
in all aspects of our lives especially our work world. Our Catholic faith
can't be siloed, but rather, it needs to be a part of the very blood and
sinew of our everyday lives. Dr. Smudde highlights the significance of uti-
lizing the gifts and talents that God has given us while staying connected
to God through daily prayer will not only yield amazing results for us
individually, but more importantly, working together as a Catholic community will reveal God's designs beyond anything we could ever fathom."

— *Dan Wagner, Government Relations Professional*

"In 2020, the world of work turned upside down with many going remote
full time. Removed from the day-to-day in my office with my team, I had
a lot more quiet time. Questions of, 'What is my purpose?', 'What do I
really do?', 'Do I have the right focus in life?', 'Do my career goals align
with the teachings of my Catholic faith or do they hinder my spiritual
growth?', became louder when the hustle and bustle of downtown Chicago retreated inside amid the COVID-19 pandemic. I needed a 'Come
to Jesus' moment professionally, and *Faithful Careers* offered the right

insights and guidance to give me renewed perspective. Through the chapters' content to the questions for meditation and suggested activities for application, I feel spiritually empowered in my career!"

— ***Kaitlin Nickrent Saldanha***, *Marketing Manager*

"This book is a must read for Catholic professionals looking to meaningfully connect their work and religious lives. The insights shared from both church leaders and accomplished experts gives a deeper understanding to how these two worlds are really one and the importance of recognizing how they build each other up. And, the best part of the book is the interactive breaks throughout that create an opportunity for personal reflection and transformation."

— ***Marrison Worthington Biel***, *Manager of Public Affairs*

"This book is a must-read for Catholics seeking a greater understanding of the role work plays in our lives and in our faith. Dr. Smudde beautifully weaves Church teaching with practical guidance for the reality of today's workplace. He demonstrates how our faith and our work can and should be united in giving glory to God, contributing to the common good, fostering personal holiness, and leading others to Christ."

— ***Kris Kranenburg***, *Catholic Speaker, Coordinator of Adult Faith Formation*

"*Faithful Careers*, by Pete Smudde, Ph.D., is an exquisite triumph giving clear direction on why and how we can hide our lives in Christ and still manage our careers. According to Dr. Smudde, the corporate world had effectively banished God from the workplace, only to discover that workers who put God first are actually more productive. Dr. Smudde's long journey and depth of research behind this book come to life as crystal clear, actionable ways we can transform our work lives into something beautiful. The application of Bible verses, papal encyclicals, commandments, virtues, the Beatitudes, and more inspire the young and old alike in completely new ways."

— ***Angela Jeffrey***, *Vice President Brand Management*

"The timing of *Faithful Careers* is ideal for those looking to transition their professional lives into something more meaningful. The global pandemic has hastened people of all faiths to make a career shift. Many have been laid off and are incredibly frustrated by Internet-driven searches that rarely land a position. For Catholics who see that ending as a potential new beginning, *Faithful Careers* provides meaningful guidance for broadening their thinking and figuring out what that next step could be. The book's organization of what, why, who, how, where, and when of integrating the Catholic faith and work, along with 'scriptural sparks' and a highly applied (vs. theological) approach, will prove beneficial for readers and seekers."

— **Sandra Duhé**, Ph.D., MBA, Southern Methodist University

"Work is an integral part of what it means to be human. God endowed each of us with the right and obligation to work even before it became a burden—whether it is work in our "career" or work in another domain. Dr. Smudde guides the reader on a journey to understand how work can often be misunderstood and how we might miss opportunities to sanctify moments of ordinary work. Dr. Smudde shares the richness of the Catholic tradition's understanding of the nature of work and offers an invitation to pause and listen to God's call on our life's work."

— **Dawn Carpenter Ph.D.**, Practitioner Fellow, Kalmanovitz Initiative for Labor and the Working Poor, Georgetown University; Host and Executive Producer, What Does It Profit? Podcast

"We don't just bring our mind and body to the workplace. We bring our spirit as well. The office, the factory, the classroom, the retail shop, the trading floor are the crucibles in which our faith is often tested, but also the ground where we pass on our values, plant seeds of hope and lay stones for the kingdom of God. The beauty of this book is that it does not approach work and faith as an abstract idea or some hoped for combination, but as a reality shared by thousands of people who seek to preach the gospel not by words but the witness of their lives. The Catholic Church has a long tradition of recognizing the spirituality of work and *Faithful Careers* explores that theological grounding while offering practical guidance for how to be a person of faith at work. A must-read for all who believe as this book shows that being religious is not incompatible with a successful career."

— **Judith Valente**, former religion correspondent for PBS-TV and author of The Art of Pausing: Meditations for the Overworked and Overwhelmed and How to Live: What The Rule of St. Benedict Teaches Us About Happiness, Meaning and Community

Faithful Careers

In *Faithful Careers* Peter M. Smudde contends that God calls us to live an "integrated life" that unifies both the spiritual and the secular aspects of life.

As an introduction to integrating the Catholic faith with one's work, this book answers, in the Catholic context, basic questions of what work is, why work is important, who we are as workers, how may we have fruitful careers, where may we find help about faith-work integration, and when we should take next steps toward better integrating our work and the Catholic faith. Smudde demonstrates how the Catholic faith truly does apply to our labor, and that our lives depend on that labor, by putting forth particular matters of the faith that pertain to faithful careers. He then puts into real-world context, pertinent teachings, concepts, principles, practices, and other means the Catholic Church provides for us, so that those lessons can be practically applied on a daily basis. Sources such as the Bible and writings of the saints, popes, contemporary Catholic spiritual writers, apologists, and scholars are applied to strengthen the support made about the book's content.

Catholic professionals at all stages of their careers will welcome this insightful book, which explores the call to put spirituality in the foreground—to obtain ever-deeper faith and, thereby, greater integration of faith in everyday life and career.

Peter M. Smudde is Professor and Associate Director of the School of Communication at Illinois State University in Normal, Illinois. He has worked for 34 years in industry and in academia (basically half the time in one and half in the other) as a professional communicator. He has been a full-time professor in higher education since 2002 and has had numerous publications, including six other books. He has a doctorate in communication and rhetoric theory from Wayne State University in Detroit, is a member of the Knights of Columbus (fourth-degree), is a member of the Pope's Worldwide Prayer Network, is a sacristan for his parish, is an Oblate in the Order of St. Benedict (Obl.OSB), and has been a leader for several years in his parish's program for the Rite of Christian Initiation of Adults (RCIA).

Dr. Smudde is available to lead workshops or speak to groups about integrating the Catholic faith with their work. He can be reached at faithful.careers@gmail.com.

Faithful Careers
Integrating the Catholic Faith and Work

Peter M. Smudde

Routledge
Taylor & Francis Group

NEW YORK AND LONDON

First published 2021
by Routledge
605 Third Avenue, New York, NY 10158

and by Routledge
2 Park Square, Milton Park, Abingdon, Oxon, OX14 4RN

Routledge is an imprint of the Taylor & Francis Group, an informa business

Library of Congress Cataloging-in-Publication Data
A catalog record for this title has been requested

ISBN: 978-0-367-69151-6 (hbk)
ISBN: 978-0-367-69150-9 (pbk)
ISBN: 978-1-003-14058-0 (ebk)

Typeset in Times New Roman
by codeMantra

To my parents, who taught my brother and me by their examples the importance of being good people, enacting a strong work ethic, and making sure the two matter as Catholics.

Contents

Prayer for Work

Creator God,
thank you for providing us
with the gift to share our talents.
Provide our community, our nation, our world
the fortitude to provide work for all
which is decent and fair.
Make us faithful stewards
of your creation
to enhance the human dignity
of our global family.
We ask this in the name of Jesus,
who lives and reigns
with you and the Holy Spirit
now and forever.
Amen

From *Being Neighbor: The Catechism and Social Justice,* USCCB, April 1998. Available online at https://www.usccb.org/prayer-and-worship/prayers-and-devotions/prayers/prayer-for-work.

About the Author

Peter M. Smudde ("smoo-dee") is Professor and Associate Director of the School of Communication at Illinois State University in Normal, Illinois. He has worked for 34 years in industry and in academia (basically half the time in one and half in the other) as a professional communicator, from technical writing to public relations. All told, he has served primarily in the automotive, communication, computer software, and higher-education industries. In this way his career has been very much a secular form of evangelization for the organizations with which he has been employed or served.

Pete has been a full-time professor in higher education since 2002 and has had numerous publications, including six other books. Because he is a university professor with industry experience in the communication field (primarily in public relations), he also has been exploring the subject of religion and spirituality in the workplace, especially for the Catholic faith.

Pete has a master's degree in writing from Illinois State University and a doctorate in communication and rhetoric theory from Wayne State University in Detroit. He is a member of the Knights of Columbus (fourth-degree and former counsel officer), is a member of the Pope's Worldwide Prayer Network, is a sacristan for his parish, is an Oblate in the Order of St. Benedict (Obl.OSB), and has been a leader for several years in his parish's program for the Rite of Christian Initiation of Adults (RCIA). He and his wife, Patty, have been married for 30 years, have two sons who are in their mid- and late twenties.

Pax.

Acknowledgments

I give thanks to almighty God for the inspiration and guidance to write this book. It has been an idea I have had for a few years, and it is so good to finally see this project come into being with God's grace. Along the way I have benefitted from the help of certain people from time to time. So, I sincerely thank Abbot Philip Davies of St. Bede Abbey in Peru, Illinois, for his spiritual formation and counsel under the *Rule* of St. Benedict; Brother Nathaniel Grossman, Director of Oblates at St. Bede Abbey, for his special interest in and prayerful and formal support of my quest for faith-career integration and this project; my fellow Oblates of St. Benedict at St. Bede Abbey for their friendship and spiritual support; Fr. Eric Powell, who is Pastor of Epiphany Catholic Parish in Normal, Illinois, for his compassion, knowledge, zeal, and humor in teaching and living the Gospels and the Catholic faith; Richard Sealy, who leads the RCIA team at Epiphany Catholic Parish, for his listening to and talking with me about this project and, especially, particular topics in this book; Brenda Snyder for her insightful counsel and guidance for my own faith-career path; Dawn Carpenter for sharing her ideas about the intersections of Catholicism, work, economics, and wealth; Judith Valente, who is a fellow Oblate of St. Benedict, for her advice about the book and encouragement on the project; Catholic students of mine with whom I have had conversations of varying depths and breadths about the faith and staying engaged in it; Illinois State University for supporting my sabbatical in the fall of 2019 to conduct research about religion and spirituality in the workplace, and this book benefitted from that research; and for all the folks at Routledge who marshaled this book into being, especially Meredith Norwich (editor), Julia Pollacco (editorial assistant and project manager), Charlie Baker (editorial assistant), Julia Hanney (production editor), Mani Kuppan (project manager for printing), and Jeno Joy (copy editor). I also sincerely thank my wife, Patty, for her love, support, and listening to me as I worked through everything to bring this book into being and for her feedback about the manuscript, and my sons, Matt and Jeff, for their interest and love.

Viva Cristo Rey!

Introduction

Faith and Work Need to be Integrated

[Jesus said,] 'Just so, your light must shine before others, that they may see your good deeds and glorify your heavenly Father.'

(Matthew 5:16)

But you, man of God, avoid all this. Instead, pursue righteousness, devotion, faith, love, patience, and gentleness. Compete well for the faith. Lay hold of eternal life, to which you were called when you made the noble confession in the presence of many witnesses.

(1 Timothy 6:11–13)

That the Catholic faith matters in work has been something I had always thought was true. I just did not have much (if any) familiarity with how. I just assumed it did and let it go at that. Over the years, maturity yielded to humility about my lack of knowledge about the Catholic faith in many respects. I even felt somewhat ashamed that, although I am a "cradle Catholic" who participated in Catholic religious-education programs from the time I was in elementary school to the time I graduated from college (only during my junior and senior years), I did not truly know as much as I thought I should about Catholicism. The desire and need to educate my sons when they were kids in the 1990s about the faith was an important start. Some time into that I decided to become a lector in my parish, and a couple of years later a resident Franciscan sister in the parish asked me to be a sponsor for someone converting to Catholicism, and I agreed. In that experience I learned a lot about the faith that I knew and did not know—and I loved it.

Over time I gradually came to want to explore more specifics. I bought Venerable Archbishop Fulton Sheen's book, *Peace of Soul* in 2010. I remembered that my parents had a copy, and after finding out more about its content, I thought I ought to read it. I did and took away much from it. Buying that book led to another and to another and to others, so now I have amassed a nice library of books and other sources about Catholicism that I have read (and am reading) over the years. All along the way the key question remained: *How may I best live the Catholic faith?* More specifically over the last ten years, especially because I joined the

Knights of Columbus, which means I must be a defender of the faith, I took seriously that role that required an answer to that key question of mine. Eventually the specific arena of living the Catholic faith at work took prominence. In 2015 I even became what I call a "lay monk" (i.e. an ordinary person who makes solemn promises to abide by a monastic rule in the world as one's station in life allows, not a consecrated/professed monk who is celibate, takes vows, and lives according to a monastic rule in a monastic community). I became an Oblate in the Order of St. Benedict because of the great overlap of the Benedictine charism (i.e. captured so succinctly in its motto, *ora et labora*, which means "prayer and work"), the *Rule* of St. Benedict, and my personal quest to integrate my work and the Catholic faith.

For the last 18 years I have been a full-time professor in higher education. For 16 years before that I was a professional communicator in industry, primarily in public relations and secondarily in technical communication. I first felt called to become a professor during my graduate studies. One of my professors told me I would be good at it, and I liked that idea because I loved learning and wanted to make a living at it. So I set three objectives for myself so that I would be credible for my future students: to work many years in the communication field, to hold a leadership position in it, and to earn a doctorate. I completed these by 2000. My wife and I decided it was time in 2002 to make the move I long wanted—felt called—to make: to become a full-time professor, specializing in public relations. My wife, too, was in the midst of a career change from marketing communication to interior design, pursuing a degree in the latter, and she was successful in that change. Our two sons were young—one just starting elementary school and the other in day care.

Part of my calling to become a professor became more apparent: To help students see and understand that the Catholic faith can be lived well and not to neglect the faith. Naturally, at this point, my formal interest in the integration of Catholicism and work began. Because I have been employed at a state university, I needed to look into the scholarly and academic literature about the intersections of religion, spirituality, and the workplace. I found tons of sources! So, in addition to my research and teaching in my field of specialization, I also have been exploring faith-work integration in general and in specific to Catholicism.

What I have learned has been astounding and glorious. *Being a religious person is not incompatible with being a working or career-oriented person.* Religion and spirituality truly always have had a role in the workplace—look at the sacred texts of at least any of the world's major religions and spiritual movements. Specifically for the Catholic faith, the topic of work is prominent in the Bible, Catholic teaching, popes, and various credible authors, from scholars and lay people to ordained clergy and professed religious. But certain sociocultural pressures, especially at least since the Industrial Revolution, have displaced or even banished religion and spirituality from the workplace.

The guiding thought in the secular, industrial context has been this: Someone is employed to get a job done, not to exercise aspects of their faith or spiritual practices. In this way work was separated from religion and spirituality rather conveniently and, presumably, for necessity so that the matters of an organization's operation and performance are the sole focal points of everyone's work so an organization can succeed. In other words, people should come to work and leave their religion and spirituality at home and in houses of worship. However, in more recent years, organizations' leaders have come to recognize that employees seek greater meaning in their work. Such greater meaning, as just the last 30-plus years' worth of literature about religion and spirituality in the workplace shows, is possible through integrating religion and spirituality in the workplace. (From August to December 2019 I had a sabbatical during which I explored this subject exclusively.)

Much of the literature about religion and spirituality in the workplace reveals that company leaders realize, when they admit people as employees or members of any sort, they are admitting whole persons—their knowledge, skills, abilities, and experiences all are accompanied and upheld by their values, beliefs, faith/spirituality, wants, needs, personality, cares, worries, and so on. For example, Ian Mitroff and Elizabeth Denton, in their watershed 1999 book, *A Spiritual Audit of Corporate America*, measured and demonstrated the vibrant and instrumental role that spiritualty and religion have in the workplace. Patricia Aburdene, in her book, *Megatrends 2010*, confirmed and amplified the role that spirituality and religion have in the workplace, further demonstrating that their intersection is no mere fad but a real and truly lasting matter of organizational survival and success that must be competently incorporated. More recent studies, such as that by the Pew Research Center in its *Religion and Public Life* project, show that people's careers are at the top of the ways people seek meaning in life, right after family. More specifically to the workplace, multiple recent studies, including those by the Society for Human Resource Management and by numerous scholars, show very clearly that a large plurality (if not a majority, depending on the study) of today's employees not only prefer to have a workplace that respects and allows for some religious/spiritual expression or inclusion, but employees perform (and, thereby, organizations perform) markedly better because of such supportive organizational cultures.

For each of us Catholics, the Catholic faith and work can and must be integrated, and there are practical ways of thinking about it, embracing it, and doing it. But there are big challenges even beyond the long-standing angst about religion in the workplace. At the outset is the difference between being *of* the world and being *in* the world. Being *of* the world, social pressures often favor polemic perspectives about matters in life that fit *either-or, yes-no, black-white* thinking. Such thinking simplifies values and decision-making because there is only one answer from between two possible choices. Combine this view with others favoring, for example, instant gratification, immediate action, self-reliance, and self-promotion (even narcissism), and there is a pattern in the secular world that privileges the self and materiality over the spiritual ethic that emphasizes other-orientation and stewardship.

> Do not love the world or the things of the world. If anyone loves the world, the love of the Father is not in him. For all that is in the world, sensual lust, enticement for the eyes, and a pretentious life, is not from the Father but is from the world. Yet the world and its enticement are passing away. But whoever does the will of God remains forever.
>
> (1 John 2:15–17)

Yet the world's expectations for success can be largely in conflict with God's expectations for holiness, especially when worldly expectations for wealth, power, honor, and pleasure are seen as ends in themselves. For example, professional conferences reveal to me (right or wrong) that people can become all too fixated on achieving esteem or prestige among their peers as something supremely important in life. This view of any field/profession is solely secular, but the Catholic faith tells me there is much more. One's successfulness or greatness in life is not due solely to one's own efforts but, rather, to God, whose graces, gifts, talents, and charisms enable someone to achieve any level of success. Ambition, then, ought to be not a matter of securing others' esteem but, rather, a matter of seeking to best fulfill God's will. Increasingly I see greater value in being a "humble worker in the Lord's vineyard," as Pope Benedict XVI once said about himself. We work in the service of God and for others. Greatness is not a matter of worldliness but, rather, holiness. "Whoever exalts himself will be humbled; but whoever humbles himself will be exalted" (Matthew 23:12). Saint Faustina Kowalska expresses a parallel sentiment in her *Diary*:

> I fervently beg the Lord to strengthen my faith, so that in my drab, everyday life I will not be guided by human dispositions, but by those of the spirit. Oh, how everything drags man towards the earth! But lively faith maintains the soul in the higher regions and assigns self-love its proper place; that is to say, the lowest one.
>
> (§210)

We can still feel good about success (without becoming prideful!), giving praise and thanksgiving to God for our being the means for revealing His glory through any successfulness. *Faithful Careers*, then, shows that being *in* (not *of*) the world fosters a more open and inclusive perspective about life—one that favors *both-and* thinking, feeling, acting, and being. Humans are not in conflict with God but, instead, in communion with God, the Father of all creation. For myself, for the greater part of my 56 years of life, I have been largely driven by secular matters. But always in the background has been divine guidance through my Catholic faith. *Faithful Careers* shows how we are called to put spirituality in the foreground—to obtain ever-deeper faith and, thereby, greater integration of my faith in daily life and vocation. "Take my yoke upon you and learn from me, for I am meek and humble of heart; and you will find rest for yourselves. For my yoke is easy, and my burden light" (Matthew 11:29–30).

There are other books about the Catholic faith and work/business, but they can be too academic by treating the subject selectively and pedantically, too specialized by applying one framework from a selected spirituality or Catholic religious orientation, or too focused on people who have many years of experience in business and industry, especially in leadership capacities. What is needed is a solid starting point, which I did not have nor could I find for my own quest. Granted, this book does not and could not cover everything about the Catholic faith and how it applies to one's work and career, and that is because I am still on my journey of learning and applying the faith myself. And who isn't? Nevertheless, *Faithful Careers* is different and valuable because it is a "primer" for how you may come to understand and integrate the Catholic faith in the very prominent aspect of your work and career in your life.

This book is meant to help Catholics fit their work in the right priorities that God expects of us so that we can fulfill His mission for us in the world—His creation, His vineyard. "Strive first for the kingdom of God" (Matthew 6:33). For when we worship God in all that we are and do, everything else falls into place. This book is not, however, a theological examination of work, which other scholarly books have done. Nor is this book focused on the big questions about or pressing issues facing Catholicism, although a few are entertained along the way. This book is meant to inspire Catholics to see (more) how the Catholic faith truly does apply to our labor and our lives that depend on that labor by showing particular matters of the faith that pertain to faithful careers. This book, then, puts into real-world context pertinent teachings, concepts, principles, practices, and other means the Catholic Church provides for us so those things can be applied in practical ways daily. Various sources, such as the Bible, writings of the saints, popes, and contemporary Catholic spiritual writers, apologists, and scholars are applied to strengthen the support made about the book's content.

Because this book is meant to be an introduction to how someone may integrate (or better integrate) the Catholic faith in their work and careers, it also does not delve into the details of economics, social justice, subsidiarity, solidarity, and other important topics, although these topics are touched upon as needed. This book also does not set out to answer all the questions about integrating the Catholic faith and work in one's career, but it does present important, foundational, and fruitful touch-points about that integration so that you can, in turn, take the next steps that suit you. Other more-advanced books specifically about the Catholic faith and business that are given in the "References and Selected Sources" list and in the "Appendix: Recommended Sources About the Catholic Faith" are good places to go to dive deeper into these topics. So, this book is the fruit of my own search for how to integrate the Catholic faith with my work and career. This book, then, is meant to start readers well on their way down a new path on their faith journey that better integrates Catholicism with their work and careers. Indeed, this book is one that I wish was available to introduce to me basic matters of faith-work integration for Catholics so, in turn, I could better explore the subject and do so more deeply through other, advanced sources thereafter and, thereby, be a better Catholic in life and in my work.

As an introduction to integrating the Catholic faith with one's work, *Faithful Careers'* content answers in the Catholic context basic questions of what work is, why work is important, who we are as workers, how may we have fruitful careers as Catholics, where may we find help about faith-work integration, and when we should take next steps toward better integrating our work and the Catholic faith. Indeed, the following six chapters address these questions in this order, because they proceed along a line of logic that each chapter (including this introduction) sets the foundation for the next so that, by the book's end, the reader is equipped to integrate the Catholic faith and her or his career, including additional resources to continue that integration. By focusing the chapters on these questions and in an approachable narrative style, this book takes a decidedly "back to basics" approach; whereas, a little coaching can go a long way to giving someone the nudge and initial guidance she or he needs to make it so. In this way, certain pronouns are used when it seems best: "I" refers to myself, "you" refers to the reader, and "we" and "us" refer to both the reader and myself and, inclusively, all Catholics, including those on the way to joining or curious about the faith. Consistent with Catholic teaching about gender, singular pronouns of "he" and "she" are used when referring to a general or named person in context.

The primary but not exclusive audience for *Faithful Careers* is Catholics (generally 18 years of age and older) who are interested in integrating the faith more into their lives and, especially, in their work and careers. Of particular interest are Catholics breaking into new careers after graduating from school, students in Newman Centers at colleges and universities, students enrolled in theology classes at Catholic high schools and Catholic colleges and universities, people enrolled in a program for the Rite of Christian Initiation of Adults (RCIA) so they may join the Catholic Church, and participants in diocesan faith-formation programs. This book would also appeal and be useful to those already well into their careers and seeking new guidance about how the Catholic faith can be instrumental in that important avenue of their lives. Additionally, this book would prove useful to Catholics who feel weary in their long careers and would appreciate (if they aren't also actively seeking) a way to revitalize themselves for the work they do through the Catholic faith. Each chapter in *Faithful Careers* begins with selected Bible verses to set the tone for its content (what I call "scriptural sparks"); then the particular topics are developed accordingly and in reasonable depth, weaving in personal stories and experiences plus focusing more on the application of principles than the theological or scholarly basis for them. The end of each chapter includes questions for meditation and suggested activities to undertake so you can be on your way to better applying the Catholic faith in your work and career.

Faithful Careers shows, as Pope St. John Paul II taught, that God calls us to live an "integrated life" that,

> In discovering and living their proper vocation and mission, the lay faithful must be formed according to the *union* which exists from their being *members of the Church and citizens of human society.…* The Second Vatican Council has invited all the lay faithful to this *unity of life* by forcefully decrying the grave consequences in separating faith from life, and the gospel from culture.… I have maintained that a faith that does not affect a person's culture is a faith 'not fully embraced, not entirely thought out, not faithfully lived.'
>
> (*Christifideles Laici*, §59; italics in original)

Indeed, Pope Francis effectively underscores John Paul II's point by saying in *Gaudete et Exsultate*,

> We are all called to be holy by living our lives with love and by bearing witness in everything we do, wherever we find ourselves.… Do you work for a living? Be holy by laboring with integrity and skill in the service of your brothers and sisters.
>
> (§14)

To *not* use God's gifts to their fullest extent to do His work and fulfill His will would be a sin. To use God's gifts without giving glory to Him and giving thanks and praise for being capable of doing so also would be sinful. The parable of the ten gold coins (Luke 19:11–27) applies especially well on this point:

> While they were listening to [Jesus] speak, he proceeded to tell a parable because he was near Jerusalem and they thought that the

kingdom of God would appear there immediately. So he said, "A nobleman went off to a distant country to obtain the kingship for himself and then to return. He called ten of his servants and gave them ten gold coins and told them, 'Engage in trade with these until I return.' His fellow citizens, however, despised him and sent a delegation after him to announce, 'We do not want this man to be our king.' But when he returned after obtaining the kingship, he had the servants called, to whom he had given the money, to learn what they had gained by trading. The first came forward and said, 'Sir, your gold coin has earned ten additional ones.' He replied, 'Well done, good servant! You have been faithful in this very small matter; take charge of ten cities.' Then the second came and reported, 'Your gold coin, sir, has earned five more.' And to this servant too he said, 'You, take charge of five cities.' Then the other servant came and said, 'Sir, here is your gold coin; I kept it stored away in a handkerchief, for I was afraid of you, because you are a demanding person; you take up what you did not lay down and you harvest what you did not plant.' He said to him, 'With your own words I shall condemn you, you wicked servant. You knew I was a demanding person, taking up what I did not lay down and harvesting what I did not plant; why did you not put my money in a bank? Then on my return I would have collected it with interest.' And to those standing by he said, 'Take the gold coin from him and give it to the servant who has ten.' But they said to him, 'Sir, he has ten gold coins.' 'I tell you, to everyone who has, more will be given, but from the one who has not, even what he has will be taken away. Now as for those enemies of mine who did not want me as their king, bring them here and slay them before me.'"

By keeping God as the top priority, we can and must recognize His investment in us and ensure a good return on that investment as a matter of our working well in His vineyard. Being religious and Catholic are compatible with all aspects of life. Faith at work and in all other aspects of life means living the Gospel that promotes human flourishing, from the individual to society. Indeed, if we remember St. James' admonition in his letter (2:14–26) that "faith of itself, if it does not have works, is dead," we truly ought to and must let our daily labor—including our labor in our careers—be a lively, genuine, and loving demonstration of the Catholic faith. The responsibilities of being a Catholic Christian, while also being a son or daughter, brother or sister, husband or wife, father or mother, uncle or aunt, friend, professional, mentor, and citizen, require balancing the secular and the spiritual.

God worked to create the earth and the cosmos. Jesus, the Word of God, worked according to God's will for our salvation. "In the beginning was the Word, and the Word was with God, and the Word was God. He was in the beginning with God" (John 1:1–2). We must work, keeping

God as our priority—to know the Word, believe in the Word, speak the Word, and act on the Word. The common ground among all Catholics is the foundation for beginning to be better at applying the faith in our lives, especially at work. *Faithful Careers*, then, builds on that foundation in particular ways. Our charge in life is to use God's gifts to us well, to live the Catholic faith ardently, and to give God glory in everything we do with and for anyone on the path of our lives. So, let us be on our way down this new path of our faith journey and, with God's grace, make it fruitful for ourselves and others.

Questions for Mediation

- What has work meant to you? Have you ever examined work as a matter for living the Catholic faith?
- In what ways can you identify whether and how the Catholic faith has ever guided you in your work and career?
- If you have ever felt uncomfortable with others when discussing religion at work, especially about matters of the Catholic faith and the Catholic Church, how did you handle it? How could you have handled it better?

Suggested Activities for Application

- Read the scriptural sparks at the start of this chapter and think about what they mean for you as a first point of departure for you to better integrate the Catholic faith and your work and career. Identify words or phrases that stand out to you, determine whether there is something to why they stand out to you and whether God is trying to tell you something, then act on it.
- Identify at least one thing you can do right away to help you on this new path of your faith journey. For example, reading the rest of this book and engaging in its content would be a good start. Even better, how about prayer—giving thanks to God for your abilities and job, asking God for guidance in doing your work well, offering your work as a kind of gift to God for all He's given you, and apologizing for times you failed God or your coworkers in your work and resolving to do better?
- Consider who in your life may be good people with whom to discuss better integrating the Catholic faith with work. Suggest opportunities to chat over coffee, a meal, a hike, or whatever seems best. Maybe use a small note pad to jot down ideas or topics that arise for further conversation or examination.

1   What Is Work?

The LORD God then took the man and settled him in the garden of Eden, to cultivate and care for it.

(Genesis 2:15)

Do not hate hard work; work was assigned by God.

(Sirach 7:15)

Do you remember your first-ever job? Mine was delivering a weekly community newspaper for which I also had to collect payment once a month. I was in middle school at the time. The responsibility, experience, and meager income I made were good for my youthful age and needs. Other jobs I held later on in my youth were similar in purpose and outcomes. In high school I worked part time in a small workout facility near my parents' home as a custodian. I later worked part time at a large nursery of trees, shrubs, flowers, and so on with a close friend of mine as a "loader," helping customers pick out and load their plants into their vehicles as well as doing other tasks as needed to keep the yard of plants and the facilities stocked and maintained. For several summers while in high school and during my college years I worked during the summers in the local school district as a custodian at a designated school or on a maintenance crew that maintained heating and air-conditioning systems in school buildings. While in college, I had a work-study job in the public affairs department of the college I attended my freshman year, was a sales associate in a retail specialty clothing store in a large shopping mall during my sophomore year, worked in the dining hall for my dorm my junior year, and worked at the front desk of the dorm in which I lived during my junior and senior years. I also held two internships, one in public relations in my senior year and one in technical writing during my graduate studies. Between my graduation with my bachelor's degree and the start of my graduate studies, I was a full-time custodian at an elementary school in the school district in which I worked in previous summers. I liked those jobs (mostly) and profited from them for as long as I held them.

While my brother and I were growing up, our dad and mom would "go to work." So, I always understood work and jobs to go together, and work was both a place where someone had a job to make money and a variety of tasks that had to be done to make that money. I felt that I was enacting this view well through my early work experiences, which, as I look back, were quite formative in my work ethic in addition to what my parents taught. Now, consider when you were young hearing adults talking about "going to work" or what they did "at work" and what impressions that left on you.

Beginning with the word, "work," we find that it has multiple definitions in any contemporary dictionary, because subtleties of context matter and it can function as other parts of speech (e.g. noun or verb). "Work" also is the root word for other words that stem from it. For a simple and secular starting point, the *Merriam-Webster Dictionary* defines "work" primarily as "to perform or carry through a task requiring sustained effort or continuous repeated operations." Likewise, the related term of "labor" can be variously defined because of its own usage patterns, and it has its own stem of derivative words. The same dictionary defines "labor" as "expenditure of physical or mental effort especially when difficult or compulsory" and as "human activity that provides the goods and services in an economy; the services performed by workers for wages as distinguished from those rendered by entrepreneurs for profits." The two words are virtually synonymous but have their own special subtleties that differentiate them and make them work well in context. As we will see, the sense and reference for the words "work" and "labor" (and their derivatives) as given here are shared in Catholic teaching. So having these terms defined gives us a solid starting point for examining the Catholic faith's intersection with them and our lives.

To examine what work is according to the Catholic faith, we need to turn to several vital sources. This chapter covers how the Bible, the *Catechism of the Catholic Church*, popes' documents of different kinds, certain Vatican publications, and lay authors' writings illuminate the subject. The idea is that these authoritative guides are useful to us for understanding what work is and its significance in our lives and the lives of others throughout the world.

The Bible

The Holy Scriptures are at the heart of the Catholic faith and, together with the Magisterium and Sacred Tradition, make up the sum of the teaching authority of the Catholic Church. A basic question is this: Where is work addressed in the Scriptures? A very interesting place to begin is the frequency with which the word "work" occurs in the Bible. According to the Vatican's statistics about words (and "tokens") used in the books of the *New American Bible* (*NAB*, revised edition), where the data are available online at http://www.vatican.va/archive/ENG0839/_INDEX.HTM, there are 1,218,577 words in the *NAB*, and the number of occurrences of the word "work" is 501. Other related words' occurrences are "worked" (40 times), "worker" (11 times), "workers" (17 times), "working" (21 times), "workingman" (1 time), "workmanship" (3 times), "workmen" (17 times), "labor" (84 times), "labored" (11 times), "laborer" (11 times), "laborers" (19 times), "laboring" (5 times), and "labors" (21 times). Add to this list "toil" (40 times), "toiled" (7 times), "toilers" (1 time), "toiling" (2 times), and "toils" (7 times). In this dataset, the total number of times in the *NAB* that work (including very related terms of labor and toil) is referenced as a concept, person, or action is 819. (Note that a very small number of the occurrences of these words are in the "Preface" and in footnotes to the books of the *NAB*, and those occurrences are indicated in the reported data given online.) As points of comparison, "pray" (and its derivatives, including "prayer") occurs 685 times, "bless" (and its derivatives, including "blessing") occurs 754 times, and "spirit" occurs 855 times. So, work is addressed throughout the Bible, and sometimes it is more prominent in certain books than in others. But the point is obvious: Work matters as much in a religious way as it does in a secular way. In fact, they necessarily intertwine, which means we must live our faith on the job as much as we do at home, at Mass, and in the community.

With the volume of occurrences of work in the Bible, a complete examination of work as it is addressed in the Bible would be a huge challenge, and it is one that is well beyond the scope of this modest book. (One example of such an undertaking is the *Theology of Work Bible Commentary*, edited by Will Messenger, which examines work in all the books of Protestant versions of the Bible.) Thematically speaking, however, work (including labor and toil) in the Bible is presented as a dignified and essential part of human activity ordained by God, the fruits of which should be enjoyed and offered up to God in thanksgiving and praise to Him. Work matters as much when done at home and for one's self and family as they do when done with and for others, ranging from helping a neighbor with a task, being a community volunteer, to working for an employer. In fact, as the first "scriptural spark" for this chapter shows, God had Adam and Eve take care of the Garden of Eden in every way, and that was before Adam and Eve's sin. Those who refrain from labor when they should be laboring are admonished for their idleness (see St. Paul's letters to the Thessalonians). People are expected to work for their own good, the good of others, and, especially, to give thanks and glory to God for what He has provided for them. In this way, work is redemptive, as we carry our individual crosses each day and follow Christ.

The Bible recognizes there are many kinds of work and people who perform the labor they do, because God, through the Holy Spirit, has given certain gifts, talents, and charisms to certain people but not others. Consider this passage from St. Paul's letter to the Romans (12:3–8):

> For by the grace given to me I tell everyone among you not to think of himself more highly than one ought to think, but to think soberly,

each according to the measure of faith that God has apportioned. For as in one body we have many parts, and all the parts do not have the same function, so we, though many, are one body in Christ and individually parts of one another. Since we have gifts that differ according to the grace given to us, let us exercise them: if prophecy, in proportion to the faith; if ministry, in ministering; if one is a teacher, in teaching; if one exhorts, in exhortation; if one contributes, in generosity; if one is over others, with diligence; if one does acts of mercy, with cheerfulness.

It is best, then, to view your life as a mission on which the Lord has called you to work in His vineyard. Doing so also requires, as Pope Francis explains in *Gaudete et Exsultate,*

> listening to God in prayer and recognizing the signs he gives you. Always ask the spirit what Jesus expects from you at every moment of your life and in every decision you make, so as to discern its place in the mission you have received. Allow the Spirit to forge in you the personal mystery that can reflect Jesus Christ in today's world.
>
> (§23)

The reason is that God desires diversity and variety among people so His will can be done and done well among everyone—provided people exercise their free will that, through some degree of discernment, supports God's will and not reject Him or His will.

Knowing that work is addressed frequently and positively throughout the Bible is comforting and liberating, as it gives us confidence in using the Bible to help us in this avenue of our lives and in our Catholic faith. In fact, using the Vatican's concordance of the number of times that "work," "labor," and "toil" (and their derivatives) occur as words in the Bible makes it easy to find passages. Just go to the Vatican's webpage for the statistics about word occurrences, look up "work," "labor," and "toil" (or any word), and see very short previews of all the Bible passages that contain them—and click on the previews to read the full passages. The "scriptural sparks" at the beginning of each chapter of this book function in a similar way—to give some direction to how work and faith in Jesus Christ combine and point the way to using them together. In fact, notice in the first scriptural spark from Genesis that work was ordained by God and essential in the Garden of Eden *before* the fall of Adam and Eve!

It is at this point that looking at the Catholic Church's teaching about work further illuminates what work is and its importance in our faith lives. There are a number of vital sources from the Church that explain to us how work and the faith interrelate and, most important, show us how what we do in our jobs and careers matters in God's vineyard. Those sources include the *Catechism,* documents popes have written and published, and documents that Vatican organizations have published.

Additionally, there lay authors who have published works that are excellent guides about integrating the faith and work.

Catechism of the Catholic Church

Formally speaking, the Catholic Church teaches well about work, its importance, and people's obligations as workers in the Lord's vineyard. The primary document for us is the *Catechism of the Catholic Church* (second edition). Created at the direction of Pope St. John Paul II in 1992 and revised at his direction in 1997 (to be in concurrence with the new Latin translation of the Bible published then), the *Catechism* is a full and complete presentation of Catholic doctrine. In this way it is a massive (920 pages), singular text that is immensely important, informative, and useful. In 2005, Pope Benedict XVI presented the *Compendium: Catechism of the Catholic Church*, which is a condensed version of the full *Catechism* but does not replace it. He did this so that anyone (believer and nonbeliever) can have a concise, more accessible, and easier point of reference about the Catholic faith that also links directly to the full *Catechism* throughout.

So if we want to know what the Catholic Church teaches about work, the best place to turn is the *Catechism*. Thanks to the *Compendium*, we can get to the fundamentals directly, then if we wish, turn to the detailed content in the full *Catechism*. The following excerpt from the *Compendium* summarizes Catholic teaching about work. (In the text excerpt below, the abbreviation "*CCC*" and the numbers that follow them refer to the *Catechism of the Catholic Church* in its full form, where there is more detail in the numbered sections about Church teaching on the given topic. The numbering scheme for topics is common in both the *Catechism* and the *Compendium* [and other Church documents] so that finding segments of any text can be done easily.)

513. What is the meaning of work?

Work is both a duty and a right through which human beings collaborate with God the Creator. Indeed, by working with commitment and competence we fulfill the potential inscribed in our nature, honor the Creator's gifts and the talents received from him, provide for ourselves and for our families, and serve the human community. Furthermore, by the grace of God, work can be a means of sanctification and collaboration with Christ for the salvation of others. (See *CCC* 2426–2428, 2460–2461.)

514. To what type of work does every person have a right?

Access to secure and honest employment must be open to all without unjust discrimination and with respect for free economic initiative and fair compensation. (See *CCC* 2429, 2433–2434.)

515. What responsibility does the State have in regard to labor?

It is the role of the State to guarantee individual freedom and private property, as well as a stable currency and efficient public services. It is also the State's responsibility to oversee and direct the exercise of human rights in the economic sector. According to circumstances, society must help citizens to find work. (See *CCC* 2431.)

516. What is the task of business management?

Business managers are responsible for the economic and ecological effects of their operations. They must consider the good of persons and not only the increase of profits, even though profits are necessary to assure investments, the future of the business, employment, and the good progress of economic life. (See *CCC* 2432.)

517. What are the duties of workers?

They must carry out their work in a conscientious way with competence and dedication, seeking to resolve controversies with dialogue. Recourse to a non-violent strike is morally legitimate when it appears to be the necessary way to obtain a proportionate benefit and it takes into account the common good. (See *CCC* 2435.)

What we see from the *Catechism* is that work is divinely ordained for us. It has great value as an important avenue for living God's law and to do so through Christ's example and teaching. In the excerpt from the *Compendium*, there are three essential dimensions to work and why it is divinely ordained. First, work is objectively valuable—it has value in and of itself and enables us, through our God-given talents, to be transformed by it, use it for others, and transcend the mere act of labor as an offering of something more to God. Second, work is subjectively valuable— it has value as a means for individual living through meeting material, economic, personal, and spiritual needs that make individuals better in the eyes of God and better caretakers of His world. Third, it is socially valuable—it has value because, through self-expression, contributions are made to and for others and the broader community that develop society and uphold matters of social justice, as work is cooperative and collaborative among many actors, from individuals to organizational entities (i.e. profit, nonprofit, governmental, nongovernmental, institutional) that are part of the social, political, and economic system. At this point it is important to turn to selected publications that recent popes have published because of the guidance they give about what work is and how it is valued.

Popes' Publications

The pope of the Roman Catholic Church is the vicar of Christ on Earth, and he is the servant of the servants of Christ. In his role, the Holy Father has supreme authority on teaching matters of Catholicism, and in this capacity he is infallible—he cannot be in error on teaching matters of the faith and morals. Documents that the pope may publish vary in their teaching authority. The supreme teaching statement a pope can make is *ex cathedra*, which means "from the chair"—that is from the Chair of St. Peter. An *ex cathedra* statement formally establishes Divinely revealed, infallible dogma, and this kind of statement has been given rarely—only twice in the history of the Catholic Church, and both were about the Blessed Mother. The pope uses other kinds of documents that advance Church teaching in various ways for various purposes (they can be seen for each pope on the Holy See's website), and these documents include papal encyclicals (i.e. the primary teaching documents popes publish), *angelus regina coeli*, apostolic constitutions, apostolic exhortations and letters, *moto proprio* statements, *urbi et orbi* and other messages for or about prominent events, homilies for Masses, prayers and daily meditations, and public speeches or remarks. Popes (especially the most recent ones) have also published books separate from these documents. Comments given in interviews with news or other mass-media organizations are another outlet for the pope to teach on matters of the faith, morals, and living the Gospels.

The authority, responsibility, and capacity for teaching, then, are vital to helping all Catholics (and, to the extent possible, all people, especially Christians) understand, embrace, and act well on the Gospels and the doctrines and dogma of the Church that Jesus Christ founded with and entrusted to St. Peter, the Apostles, and their successors. In the Church's earliest time, as *Acts of the Apostles* shows, St. Peter and the Apostles engaged in many discussions and decisions (with St. Peter making the final decision) about doctrines, dogma, practices, and other necessary matters for establishing Christ's church that would be open to all—to be universal or catholic for all peoples. Since then, the Catholic Church has grown and continued to advance and be organized to handle all respects for the salvation of humanity in the entire world. The importance of work in the lives of the Catholic faithful is as prominent as other matters of the Church. In this way, then, popes have issued various publications about or that pertain to work and its role and importance in the lives of the faithful and all humanity. Three categories of papal publications are worth reviewing because of the centrality of work in them: (1) those about the "apostolate" of the laity, (2) those focused on work and labor, and (3) those about society, wherein work is vital. The following three subsections very simply summarize selected contributions in these categories of documents with you should become familiar.

Laity

Ordained priests and deacons are clergy in the Catholic Church, and those who have made permanent vows are members of Catholic religious orders (e.g. monks and nuns). All others are considered "lay" members (or "laity") of the Church, denoting that their secular station in life is different from Catholic clergy and religious. All members of the Catholic Church make up the Body of Christ in His Church. The "apostolate" (i.e. special ministry that serves the Church's mission) of ordained and professed religious people is specifically to lead and administer Church teaching and fulfill duties to humanity and society. Priests are specially ordained—being in the person of Christ—to administer the sacraments and serve at the Holy Mass, and they have the pastoral responsibility for the faith development of the people in their parishes and fulfill other duties according to their bishops and their vocation. The apostolate of the laity, in its own way, lives the Gospel and upholds the doctrines of the Catholic Church in people's daily, secular lives in the world. Priests, deacons, monks, and nuns also do this but they also fulfill their duties and responsibilities as Catholic clergy in the world, especially if they are members of a particular religious order.

To provide specific guidance for the laity, at least three papal documents are important to know and, most important, pertain to the relationship of work with the Catholic faith. First is *Apostolicam Actuositatem*, which was promulgated during the Second Vatican Council (Vatican II). This document is a decree about the importance of the laity in the life of the Body of Christ, the Catholic Church. Being a member of that body means, as Edward Hahnenberg explains in *A Concise Guide to the Documents of Vatican II*, all members of the Catholic Church "share in the prophetic, priestly, and kingly work of Christ by evangelizing, sanctifying, and witnessing to others" (p. 104). *Apostolicam Actuositatem* addresses many ways the laity are essential to the Church's life within the confines of secular affairs. In this way, the laity are vital contributors to God's mission both in the world and in the Church.

The second document is *Gaudium et Spes*, which also came from Vatican II. This document addresses how the Church will serve pastorally in the world. Beginning with human dignity as the link between the Church and the world, this document explains how the "signs of the times" (i.e. particular aspects of the modern world, from changing attitudes to advancing technology) affect social, moral, and religious facets of humanity that threaten change for the worse in many ways and for the better in other ways. Chapter 3 especially focuses on human activity and, most important, on work as the extension of God's creation of the cosmos, and that human activity of work performed out of love should be for the benefit of all people.

The third document is *Christifideles Laici*, which is Pope St. John Paul II's apostolic exhortation about the laity's vocation and mission in the Church and the world. This subject was the heart of the 1987 Synod of Bishops, and this document is the pope's formal response to and synthesis of the bishops' findings and recommendations. *Christifideles Laici*, which is a special document we will return to several times in this book, reaffirms the content of the preceding two documents from Vatican II and advances more guidance about the ways the laity contribute to the life of the Church and the welfare of humanity in the world, especially through their labor in the secular dimensions of life, which also should enact the Gospels' messages and fulfill the Church's mission.

Work and Labor

The Industrial Revolution, in historical terms, spanned roughly from the mid-1700s to the start of World War I. During the latter half of that period a "technological revolution" emerged that was sparked by great advancements in manufacturing and production technology. These advancements were instrumental to the creation and proliferation of telegraph networks, railroads, gas and water supply systems, sewage systems, electrical power grids, and telephone networks. Economic growth skyrocketed, living standards improved greatly among certain nations, productivity rose, and prices for goods fell dramatically. But at the same time unemployment rates rose sharply as machines replaced workers and some avenues for commerce and industry died out or underwent vast changes. The results also included widespread social conflict, giving rise to the ideologies of socialism and communism that were framed as cor-rectives for the adverse effects of capitalism and industrialization during that time.

It is this context that inspired Pope Leo XIII to write and publish *Rerum Novarum* in 1891 for the Church and the world. This encyclical has proven over the ensuing decades to be a watershed for Catholic social doctrine and teaching, spawning multiple documents from succeeding popes, as will be shown shortly. Key points in the document concern (1) the role of the state as promoting social justice and the role of the Church to speak out on social issues that ensure harmony and protect the poor, (2) private property rights as vital and natural because of (at least) God's granting of particular gifts and talents to people but not others, and people capitalize on those gifts and talents, (3) market forces that must be tempered by moral considerations to keep unrestricted capitalism in check, and (4) employer and employees having duties to one another, and trade unions and collective bargaining can be alternatives to state inter-vention in that relationship to ensure the rights, respect, dignity, com-pensation, and protections of workers.

To Pope St. John Paul II, *Rerum Novarum* was so important that he wrote and published two encyclical letters (one on its 90th anniversary and one on its 100th anniversary) and focused greatly on work and work-ers. The first letter, *Laborem Exercens*, affirms the relevance of *Rerum Novarum*'s place in contemporary times. In particular, *Laborem Exercens* argues aggressively for the dignity and rights of workers and the labor they undertake for employers and society. It also advocates for effective ways to resolve conflict between employees and employers that befit the times and needs. Finally, the document explains the spiritual dimension to work that finds its basis in Christ. As St. John Paul says,

> Let the Christian who listens to the word of the living God, uniting work with prayer, know the place that his work has not only in *earthly progress* but also in *the development of the Kingdom of God,* to which we are all called through the power of the Holy Spirit and through the word of the Gospel.
>
> (§27; italics in original)

It is easy to see how *Laborem Exercens* prefigured and likely was the philosophical-theological basis for the fall of communism in 1989.

Pope John Paul II's second encyclical letter, *Centesimus Annus,* presents a "re-reading" of *Rerum Novarum* in light of how its content newly illuminates on the times 100 years later and for the future. *Centesimus Annus* explains that, although many things have changed, including communism's fall in 1989, the fundamental messages of *Rerum Novarum* remain crucial. Indeed, greater conscientious and moral effort must be made to protect human dignity and rights, especially for the poor. Ever-expanding technological advancements pose particularly active areas for ensuring sociocultural, moral, economic, plus ecological and environmental protections for individuals, companies, communities, nations, and the world—all of which must work in harmony in God's vineyard.

> For this [organizing of a solid economy that would direct the market's functioning toward the common good] to happen, *a great effort must be made to enhance mutual understanding and knowledge, and to increase the sensitivity of consciences....* But to accomplish this, the poor—be they individuals or nations—need to be provided with realistic opportunities. Creating such conditions calls for a *concerted worldwide effort to promote development,* an effort which also involves sacrificing the positions of income and of power enjoyed by the more developed economies.
>
> (52; italics in original)

Underscoring so many of the points in these three important documents, Pope Francis, on at least two occasions, stressed matters about the dignity and value of work. In his *Address* to the Christian Union of Business Executives on October 31, 2015, Pope Francis reiterated a point from his apostolic exhortation, *Evangelii Gaudium,* that

> The vocation of a businessperson is, in fact, 'a noble vocation, provided that those engaged in it see themselves challenged by a greater

meaning in life; this will enable them truly to serve the common good by striving to increase the goods of this world and to make them more accessible to all.'

(§203)

Pope Francis went further in his *Address* to explain the importance of work and workplaces being "places of sanctification, through each person's commitment to building fraternal relationships among businesspeople, executives and employees, fostering co-responsibility and cooperation in common interests" (§4). Business' place in society is for the good of all by advancing economic development, innovation, and employment—as long as the center of business is the person and not money.

Society

Popes, especially over the last 130 years, have been astutely aware of the fragility of society and the Catholic Church's (indeed, all peoples') responsibility to recognize that fragility, embrace the importance of strengthening society, and take prudent and moral action that upholds human dignity, applies lessons from the Gospels, and allows for advances in ways that improve the world for all. Popes have produced documents over this time, beginning with *Rerum Novarum,* that present particular advances in Catholic social teaching. Because work is a vital part of both individuals and society, work has figured prominently in this big-picture context.

Pope Pius XI, in his 1931 document, *Quadragesimo Anno,* which celebrated the 40th anniversary of *Rerum Navarum,* addressed the need to ensure the sanctity of the social order, especially in the wake of the end of World War I and worldwide economic depression that had begun. In the document the core topics of private property, capital and labor, social order, and communism and socialism parallel *Rerum Novarum* and extend it by calling for greater efforts to combat the evils from unrestrained economic power. Pope Pius teaches that

> it is no less evident that, had not God the Creator of all things, in keeping with His goodness, first generously bestowed natural riches and resources—the wealth and forces of nature—such supreme efforts would have been idle and vain, indeed could never even have begun. For what else is work but to use or exercise the energies of mind and body on or through these very things? And in the application of natural resources to human use the law of nature, or rather God's will promulgated by it, demands that right order be observed. This order consists in this: that each thing have its proper owner. Hence it follows that unless a man is expending labor on his own property, the

labor of one person and the property of another must be associated, for neither can produce anything without the other.

(§53)

Pope St. John XXIII issued *Mater et Magistra* in 1961, on the 70th anniversary of *Rerum Novarum*, in large measure to confirm the Church's role as both mother and teacher for the world. The core idea is that human dignity must be promoted through true community collaboration based on charity, not self-interest, especially in economic matters. In both social and economic terms, Pope John explains, work

> must be regarded not merely as a commodity, but as a specifically human activity. In the majority of cases a man's work is his sole means of livelihood. Its remuneration, therefore, cannot be made to depend on the state of the market. It must be determined by the laws of justice and equity. Any other procedure would be a clear violation of justice, even supposing the contract of work to have been freely entered into by both parties.

(§18)

His point extends into the national and international arenas where social justice ensures economic activity is pursued for the common good and not merely for private gain. The document acknowledges many advances and changes in the world since *Rerum Novarum* was published, and it advances important points about the "common good," which balances interests and needs between society and economy; agriculture and agricultural work as dignified and essential to balance against industry and the expansion of urban settings; and international assistance to nations that have not advanced as well as industrialized nations.

In Pope St. Paul VI's *Populorum Progressio*, issued in 1967, he argues that the fundamental purpose of the world's economy is to serve all people and not just a few of them. The separation between rich nations and poor nations, in combination with flareups of social unrest, has gotten ever wider. God created the world to provide everyone—not just some people—with the necessities of life. Those with wealth have a moral obligation to help those with little or no wealth. In the world socio-economic context, wealthy nations must provide aid for and join in solidarity with poor/developing nations; trade relations between wealthy and poor nations must be established, fair, and strong; and all nations regardless of wealth must not only commit but also act in accordance with charity to build a humane world community. Pope Paul explains that work

> is something willed and approved by God. Fashioned in the image of his Creator, 'man must cooperate with Him in completing the work of creation and engraving on the earth the spiritual imprint which he

himself has received.' God gave man intelligence, sensitivity and the power of thought—tools with which to finish and perfect the work He began. Every worker is, to some extent, a creator—be he artist, craftsman, executive, laborer or farmer.... It is directed to the establishment of a supernatural order here on earth, a task that will not be completed until we all unite to form that perfect manhood.

(§28)

In celebration of *Populorum Progressio*'s 20th anniversary, Pope St. John Paul II released *Sollicitudo Rei Socialis*, which addressed two problems facing stronger social development in the world: that of the Third World's failed development and the need to embrace solidarity as a framework for both lasting peace and human dignity, particularly for the poor. People and nations are necessarily interdependent and, therefore, need to thrive through fair and effective collaboration. Beginning with attention on the neediest people of the world, solidarity can lift their social and economic positions collaboratively with wealthier individuals' and nations' help. Pope John Paul shows that

According to Sacred Scripture therefore, the notion of development is not only 'lay' or 'profane,' but it is also seen to be, while having a socio-economic dimension of its own, the modern expression of an essential dimension of man's vocation.

(§30)

He also reasserts that "it is always man who is the protagonist of development" (§30) and turns to the Church Fathers for their "optimistic vision of history and work, that is to say of the perennial value of authentic human achievements, inasmuch as they are redeemed by Christ and destined for the promised Kingdom" (§31).

Caritas in Veritate, Pope Benedict XVI's encyclical letter written in 2009, addresses the global dimensions about achieving the common good, discussing matters of economics and social issues such as hunger, environment, migration, sexual tourism, bioethics, cultural relativism, social solidarity, energy, and population. In it he explains intersections between human pursuits and the environment, leaning on charity and truth as the critical, moral links among justice, the common good, and human development. In this way the pope emphasizes that both governments and private markets have limitations and responsibilities to balance the needs and wants of all, calls out prevailing ideologies on the right and left to focus on what is good for all, and exhorts all people to think and act with love and truth as moral foundations to all human endeavors to ensure that all facets of the global society are addressed, especially through the leaders and organizations focused on political, business, religious, financial, and aid dimensions of life. Pope Benedict explains that

Business activity has a human significance, prior to its professional one. It is present in all work, understood as a personal action, an '*actus personae*,' which is why every worker should have the chance to make his contribution knowing that in some way 'he is working 'for himself.' With good reason, Paul VI taught that 'everyone who works is a creator.' It is in response to the needs and the dignity of the worker, as well as the needs of society, that there exist various types of business enterprise, over and above the simple distinction between 'private' and 'public.' Each of them requires and expresses a specific business capacity (§41).

Pope Francis' encyclical letter, *Laudato Si'*, published in 2015, is addressed to "every person living on this planet" (§3), so that we all may engage in an inclusive dialog that bears fruit about the future of Earth. The matter of our planet's environmental fragility and decay is paramount, and a new path must be cut and followed to preserve our common home now and for ages to come—it is our duty as the Earth's caretaker. In this document Pope Francis cites consumerism that promotes rampant materiality, the "throwaway culture" that extends from unwanted things to unwanted people, and irresponsible development that squanders resources as instrumental in the degrading of the environment and the increasing warming of the planet. What is needed is a holistic, global response that reverses the breakdown of society and the planet. Pope Francis reminds us that work and business in general is "a noble vocation, directed at producing wealth and improving our world" (§129). Moreover, he explains that,

> If we reflect on the proper relationship between human beings and the world around us, we see the need for a correct understanding of work; if we talk about the relationship between human beings and things, the question arises as to the meaning and purpose of all human activity. This has to do not only with manual or agricultural labour [*sic*] but with any activity involving a modification of existing reality, from producing a social report to the design of a technological development. Underlying every form of work is a concept of the relationship which we can and must have with what is other than ourselves.... Work should be the setting for this rich personal growth, where many aspects of life enter into play: creativity, planning for the future, developing our talents, living out our values, relating to others, giving glory to God.

> (§125, 127)

Two and a half years later, Pope Francis wrote and shared a letter to the participants in the international conference, "From *Populorum Progressio* to *Laudato Si'*." This letter is a very brief statement about human and social development since 1967, builds a bit on *Laudato Si'*, and is focused on the future. His emphasis is on the value of work, including efforts to organize workers for their protection from abuse. Pope Francis says that work "is more than a mere doing; it is above all, a mission," because work is our collaboration "with the creative work of God, ... when by our activity we give sustenance to our families and response to the needs of our neighbor" (§3). We all must guard against falling into the temptations of (1) "collectivist individualism" that only privileges one's self and interests without regard for the welfare of others outside one's circle of family and friends, (2) "the cancer of corruption" that undermines the moral and ethical foundations for any human activity and converts matters to evil, and (3) "educating consciences in solidarity, respect and care" that leans on virtues to spur significant improvements across all strata of society and the natural world (§14–16).

Amidst the worldwide COVID-19 pandemic in 2020, Pope Francis wrote and published his encyclical, *Fratelli Tutti*. It is a document that emphasizes that we are sisters and brothers because we are children of God, the one Creator. Fraternity and social friendship are central among all people at all times, from ordinary living to acute times of hardship, and they are essential so the world can truly be more just and at peace. The ways that we are interconnected in this world are so vast and vital that only by working together can we achieve the kind of lasting peace and care that is so necessary for our and the planet's survival. Love is the key to dismantling the structures in our social, economic, and political systems that perpetuate injustice, indifference, selfishness, racism, poverty, unemployment, violations of rights, and other evils. Charity, which subsumes both private life and public order, "calls for an effective process of historical change that embraces everything: institutions, law, technology, experience, professional expertise, scientific analysis, administrative procedures, and so forth" (§164) because the public order protects domestic, private life. From this principle of love, Francis prescribes (§112, §115) the tools of benevolence (i.e. truly wanting what is best for others and their well-being) and solidarity (i.e. caring for and serving others and not ideologies to fight against evils in the world). To Pope Francis, employment is "the biggest issue" because

> In a genuinely developed society, work is an essential dimension of social life, for it is not only a means of earning one's daily bread, but also of personal growth, the building of healthy relationships, self-expression and the exchange of gifts. Work gives us a sense of shared responsibility for the development of the world, and ultimately, for our life as a people.
>
> (§162)

From the vitality of work to the need to eradicate evil and destructive attitudes and structures, love is at the heart of and is the enabler of all things among all peoples.

> Only a gaze transformed by charity can enable the dignity of others to be recognized and, as a consequence, the poor to be acknowledged and valued in their dignity, respected in their identity and culture, and thus truly integrated into society.
>
> (§187)

Vatican Documents

There are many councils, commissions, offices, and various other groups within the Catholic Church that have specific charters to attend to particular arenas of Church and human affairs. Each group may produce documents of varying types and lengths that cover matters that fall under their charters. One council that is especially important to the subject of work is the Pontifical Council for Justice and Peace. This council was created through Vatican II and has evolved somewhat since then. Its mission was and remains

> to aim at ensuring that justice and peace are promoted in the world according to the Gospel and the social doctrine of the Church.... [and is committed] to deepening and spreading the social doctrine of the Church, especially with regard to the world of work.
>
> (*Annuario Pontificio,* 2019, §9–10)

In 2016, under Pope Francis' order, the council became one of several organized under the Dicastery for Promoting Integral Human Development. According to its website, the dicastery "deals specifically with issues concerning migrants, refugees and victims of slave trade [and] human trafficking, giving necessary attention to issues pertaining to the needs of those who are forced to abandon their countries or those who are without one" (§3).

Among the documents published by the Pontifical Council for Justice and Peace, two are particularly worth noting for their treatment of the subject of work. The first is *Compendium of the Social Doctrine of the Church*, published in 2004 at the direction of Pope St. John Paul II. The document is a thorough treatment of Catholic social teaching, and it is meant also to be "a precise but complete overview" of that teaching (p. xxi). Its 12 chapters are divided among three parts that, building upon and advancing beyond the content of the prior papal documents summarized in the previous section, address doctrines about the Church's enactment of Christ's mission, humans and human rights, family in society, work and the economy, national and political communities, the environment, peace in the world, pastoral responsibilities, and the role and duties of the laity. Chapter 6 specifically covers human work, beginning with the Bible's treatment of the subject, treating Jesus' life as a worker, and the value of, dignity of, duties for, and rights to work. The chapter also addresses the solidarity among workers as well as contemporary matters of work in the world and the economy. Chapter 7 delves into the larger picture of how laborers, businesses, societies, and economies intersect, emphasizing that all must in charity be in service to the good of humanity and taking good care of God's creation through prudent and moral application of human and natural resources.

The second document from the Pontifical Council for Justice and Peace is *Vocation of the Business Leader*, which was first published in 2011, following conferences about how Pope Benedict XVI's encyclical, *Caritas in Veritate*, can be applied, especially to business. This document, which is in its fifth edition and published in 2018 by the dicastery and not the council, includes updated content that covers teaching from Pope Francis about the environment and the noble vocation of business. The document is meant to be a usable and used handbook for people in business so they may *see* how work can be done in tune with Catholic social teaching, *judge* well on business decisions of all kinds, and *act* in ways that demonstrate the viability, prudence, and wisdom of Church teaching that pertains to business in the service of God.

Lay Authors' Writings

In recent years many lay authors have written well about how work and the Catholic faith intertwine, and a predominant medium for their writings is digital publications, such as *Catholic Stand, Integrated Catholic Life*, and others. Additional media include academic publications, organizations like the Fellowship of Catholic Scholars, and of course books. The "References and Selected Sources" list at this book's end shows the output of some lay authors that I have found to be especially informative and useful.

Looking across the lay authors' publications, there are important topics and concepts that are worth highlighting. First is the unequivocal observation of and advice about the natural and necessary integration of the Catholic faith and work. All authors show ways that the Bible plus Catholic teaching from the popes, the *Catechism*, and Church councils all provide clear guidance about work in all respects. In this way there is a definitive theology and sound practical counsel about work that all Catholics can understand, embrace, and apply daily. Our work is in the service of God, not mammon or money. Money is a means for economic transactions, and the work we do is far more spiritually and religiously valuable because our work is simultaneously meant to be conducted in the stewardship of God's creation and for the common good of others locally and globally. Material goods, or mammon, are temporary and meant to be means for living, not the things for which we live. Detachment from the material world is necessary so that we can live a holy life by taking up our cross and following Jesus in all that we are and do (see Luke 14:25–33). Community, which spans from family and friends to businesses and society, is part of an economic system that functions well and *morally* for the common good of humanity and human freedom. In these sources and those that apply St. Benedict's *Rule*, which interlocks prayer with work as the two both give worship to God, we understand that through our work we give glory to God with the resources of His creation, using the talents and gifts He has given us. We also find God in what we do and Jesus in the people with whom we work and meet.

The second topic among lay authors is that work involves a vocation, a calling from God to make use of the gifts He's given each person. Discernment of that calling is key—to understand what God is saying, not whether or not God is speaking. Free will matters greatly in discernment, making sure to distinguish between self-wants and divine direction and going down the avenue that would best suit your vocation in God's vineyard according to your gifts and talents *and* to follow Christ in what you do in the giving of yourself—to fulfill God's will and lead others to Heaven. In this way, for example, your career may include certain changes in the work (e.g. kind, place, scope, difficulty, people) you do. Changes from working in one industry to another, such as from working in a corporation to becoming a full-time academic (which is my humble experience), can be the case in your career. Alternatively, small or even no changes may be the best route, as God would have you continue in your present state of affairs (i.e. maintain stability) to better prepare you for something to come. Recognize, though, a career is not the focus of work but, rather, a career is the sum of all of your experiences (from projects completed to positions held) to do certain work that engages your gifts that bring glory to God.

Effective discernment is instrumental in the making of your career (and living your life) as you listen for and reflect on how God is guiding you. The first letter from St. John addresses discernment this way:

> Beloved, do not trust every spirit but test the spirits to see whether they belong to God, because many false prophets have gone out into the world. This is how you can know the Spirit of God: every spirit that acknowledges Jesus Christ come in the flesh belongs to God, and every spirit that does not acknowledge Jesus does not belong to God.
>
> (1 John 4:1–3)

Discernment involves making careful sense of what God wants us to be and do and then making sound decisions about that. Discernment may include prayer, contemplation, scripture, the sacraments, and spiritual direction from a qualified guide. Writing for a lay audience and using St. Ignatius of Loyola's spiritual exercises, Fr. Timothy Gallagher, in his book *Discerning the Will of God*, explains that discernment is a process. It begins with the knowledge that God loves us deeply and desires our communion with Him, and we must be intellectually, emotionally, and genuinely open to His will and love.

Fr. Gallagher explains that three "modes" for discernment can be at play, where active engagement of the mind, soul, and heart with any or all of them is essential to be able to recognize important patterns and make good sense of them and identify God's will and experience His love. First, there may be such clarity about what to be or do that there can be no doubt, as the clarity of the choice to be made is a direct gift from God. Second, there can be a recurring or consistent pull of the spirit toward one particular way of being or doing, as God draws us little by little toward one option. And third, upon a sufficiently thorough collection and scrutiny of information (e.g. positives vs. negatives, advantages, vs. disadvantages, risks vs. benefits), a preponderance of data seems to favor one option over others or, perhaps, if more than one option seems "equally" meritorious, there is freedom to pursue the option that would best reveal God's glory. Discernment, then, yields insights and revelation about God's will, personal fulfillment in having employed free will to make a good decision, and a perspective for how you may fulfill God's will and experience His love. And remember: God is love, and if anything does not promote love, it is not from God.

The third common topic among lay authors is human dignity, which entails protection and respect of all workers. Every person has the right to work—to use their God-given talents and gifts in the best ways that their discernment has revealed. From top management to entry-level positions of any kind, workers must be in solidarity with one another to ensure the protection and respect they deserve as humans and God's laborers in His vineyard. Subsidiarity, which is the delegation of responsibility and accountability to the lowest and most appropriate level to get things done, is key. At no time should any worker endure any immoral, unreasonable, unlawful, or other untoward treatment, assignments, working conditions, compensation, or other aspects. Fundamentally, human dignity in work requires charity (love) and involves the Good person doing well in their work and in business. This point entails that both employers and employees operate virtuously, which at least would mean everyone lives and works *prudently* (i.e. a moral sense about good and evil, especially in the service of the love of God), *temperately* (i.e. through the discipline of the desires to serve the command to love), *justly* (i.e. give to each person what is their due), and with *fortitude* (i.e. courage or constancy in the pursuit of the good). Leadership and business management are examined among lay authors (see especially publications about applying St. Benedict's *Rule* in which both prayer and work are necessarily combined) because it is vital to ethical, effective, and efficient organizational operations and organizational and employees' success.

Even so, we know that sometimes we will endure suffering in our work, perhaps because a boss is a poor manager/leader or one's capabilities just are not up to par because of sickness or need for education, remediation, or reassignment. Perhaps suffering comes from an ill-tempered person who subverts your work or slanders you behind your back. In any case, suffering of any sort is temporary, and, along with prayers for the people/perpetrators involved, it should be offered up to God in communion with Christ's suffering on the Cross, which He did to redeem our sins. Remember what Jesus said in Matthew (10:38): "...whoever does not take up his cross and follow after me is not worthy of me." However, when suffering stems from immoral, unreasonable, unlawful, or other untoward reasons, action must be taken to alleviate and eliminate it justly and expediently. The emphasis on human dignity plus solidarity among laborers, the principle of subsidiarity, and the cardinal virtues of justice, prudence, temperance, and fortitude are instrumental in ensuring a good workplace.

The fourth topic among lay authors is apologetics, which means to defend the Catholic faith and do so out of love. Have you experienced times at your job (or anywhere) that certain issues came up and you wondered how the Catholic faith applies? Or have you heard people discuss or been in interpersonal conversations about matters of the Catholic Church that pertain to work or not? The main point that the lay authors make about apologetics is to be not afraid. Engage in conversation to the best of your ability and with love, and if you find you cannot provide your listener(s) with sufficient and authoritative information, offer to get it and then give it to them later, offering further conversation then. In any case, it helps to have more and better knowledge about the Catholic faith and Catholic teaching.

Certainly, numerous resources are available specifically about Catholic apologetics, and selected titles have been included in this book's "References and Selected Sources" list and, especially, the Appendix. The sources covered in just this chapter can be helpful as well. Enrolling in a RCIA (Rite of Christian Initiation of Adults) program or other religious formation program at your or a local Catholic parish or in your diocese can help greatly in this regard too. For myself, the whole experience of learning about the Catholic faith has been and is interesting, engaging, enriching, and inspiring. I am ever thankful that I have made the effort to learn and continue to learn about the Catholic faith so that I can improve myself and others, even if they are not Catholic. Being a good example in and at work of how to live the Catholic faith matters in words *and* actions.

Conclusion

So, what is work? Dictionary definitions of the word and concept, including its counterpart terms, labor and toil, get at its basic sense and reference. But to us Catholics, it is more. Work is ordained by God. It is dignified and natural, as we each work in His vineyard of the world that He created. It serves as a means to serve, thank, and praise God for His creation and His gifts to us individually. As St. Benedict teaches us in his *Rule*, prayer interlocks with work, as both are necessary means for living and as a sanctified act of worship of God.

Indifference to work or idleness scoffs at labor's importance in all these facets. Indifference or idleness, then, puts one's self above others by withdrawing from making contributions to the common good. In the other extreme, overwork (perhaps being required by an employer to work more than is reasonable) or workaholism also severs the vital ties between the sanctity of labor so that mammon is served excessively more over God and the common good. Rest is needed to revitalize both physically and spiritually so that, when refreshed, we can reengage in that which God has called us—to a vocation that brings glory to God through the work we do for ourselves and others with what He has given us.

Work makes us participants, caretakers, and even cocreators and collaborators with God for His creation, as we apply our God-given talents and gifts to the earthly resources to, in turn, contribute to the common good for humanity. Love must guide us in our work and our laboring with and for others. Through the solidarity of all workers with one another and by applying the principle of subsidiarity, our work energizes society and economies that enrich individuals and communities of all scales. Through work done with love and in accordance with the cardinal virtues of prudence, temperance, justice, and fortitude, wealth that is amassed more by some can and should be shared with those poor in wealth so that they may be "lifted up"—be more engaged in the improvement of their own and others' social, economic, and spiritual positions.

Questions for Mediation

- How has your thinking about work been changing or enlarging so far? What topics would you like to explore more?
- What specific ways (little ways to start, if you wish) would you offer up your work any day as acts of worship to God? Beginning with a heartfelt prayer, how would you do that?
- Which ideas from this chapter stand out to you as "tools" or inspiration to begin your greater integration of work with the Catholic faith?

Suggested Activities for Application

- If you don't have a copy of the newest translation of the Catholic Bible (the *NAB* is particularly helpful because of its extensive notes) and the latest edition of the *CCC* (and/or the *Compendium* for the *Catechism*), you truly should get them because they are vital sources for all matters of the Catholic faith and how to live it. Examine its treatment about the importance and dignity of work.

- Obtain online one or more of the papal and Vatican sources introduced in this chapter (http://w2.vatican.va/content/vatican/en.html, then search for them by title) or in printed form from a book seller, so you may explore them and refer to them as needed. See the "References and Selected Sources" list later in this book.

- Check out a few publications by lay authors to learn about the interconnections between work and the faith. (See the "References and Selected Sources" list or search on your own on the internet.) Look for key take-aways that intrigue you or enrich what you are coming to know and desiring to apply from the Catholic faith in your work.

2   Why Is Work Important?

There is nothing better for mortals than to eat and drink and provide themselves with good things from their toil. Even this, I saw, is from the hand of God. For who can eat or drink apart from God?

(Ecclesiastes 2:24–25)

Do not let anyone have any food if he refuses to do any work. Now we hear that there are some of you who are living in idleness, doing no work themselves but interfering with everyone else's. In the Lord Jesus Christ, we order and call on people of this kind to go on quietly working and earning the food that they eat. My brothers, never grow tired of doing what is right.

(2 Thessalonians 3:10–13)

Back to my very first job delivering a weekly community newspaper. My motive for it was to earn money so I could buy things I wanted (even saving money for things later) without bothering my parents for money. My parents also opened savings accounts for my brother and me, so we would learn to save money and use it well. I found out about the newspaper-delivery job from a friend, contacted the publisher's representative to ask to be a delivery boy for it, and did it for many months. The work was not the most engaging, but it was simple and what I could handle. After the stacks of papers were delivered to my parents' home by early afternoon, I had to bind each of them myself with a rubber band and load as many as I could (using ropes to keep the load secure) into a red Radio Flyer wagon that I tied to and pulled from the back of my bicycle. Then, because the starting point of my route was over a half mile from my neighborhood, I rode with my load of papers to deliver them to all the houses on my route. Because my wagon could only carry so much, I had to make two trips, and the wagon was embarrassingly noisy when it was empty on my way home to get more papers and when I finished my route. As a community newspaper, it was not subscription-based, and every house on my route got a copy. Once a month I had to stop at each house and ask for a fixed sum to pay for the paper, which the home's occupant could pay or deny. Because the paper was not subscription-based, many people did not feel the need to pay for it because they did not ask for it. Even so, I would get a share of the earnings from my route for my work, and that pay was helpful. The better my service in delivering papers to people and the genuinely nicer I was, the more I earned.

My motive for my first job was simple enough, and that motive was largely behind why I sought other jobs after it. It is interesting how earning money (earning it to spend and to save and manage) seemed to be the primary motive but enlarged to include others. Another important factor was obtaining degrees of independence over the years of my youth, which was a characteristic teenage desire. As I grew older and sought to establish a respectable work record after high school, additional factors about the benefits of work also became important such as being involved in something that was interesting or exciting that is bigger than myself, learning new skills and extending existing ones, building relationships with other people, and making contributions that matter to other people for their own lives.

Why do we work? What were your motivations for work over the years, from your first job to those of your career? The scriptural sparks for this chapter certainly point to the fulfillment of basic needs, but they also imply a higher level of importance to work being a divine mission for people given by God. Let us first look to Jesus as an ordinary worker and then examine social pressures, religion and spirituality in the workplace, encountering challenges to faith, and acedia's threat to working well in the Lord's vineyard.

Jesus the Worker

From the practical to the philosophical, why we work matters a lot. The seeds for wanting or needing to work are planted in the soil of our domestic environments when we are young. The care and cultivation of attitudes toward and motives for work ideally bear good fruit as we grow. Like us, Jesus learned and knew about the value of work. Venerable Archbishop Fulton Sheen, in his book, *The Life of Christ*, explains how Jesus identifies with us, because

> The human family has its trials; so He sanctified them by living in a family. Labor and work done by sweat of the brow were humanity's lot; therefore He, 'the Son of Man,' became a carpenter. No single human affliction which befalls man as a result of sin escaped His oneness with it. 'He took away our illnesses and lifted our diseases from us' (Matthew 8:17).

> (p. 196)

Archbishop Sheen adds more detail about the "hidden" 30 years of Jesus' upbringing as an ordinary laborer under his foster father, St. Joseph, and then changing careers to fulfill God's design:

> He lived under a humble roof, obedient to His parents. For eighteen uneventful years He fixed the flat roofs of Nazarene homes and

mended the wagons of the farmers. Every mean and lowly task was part of the Father's business.... Justin Martyr, basing himself on tradition, says that during this time Our Lord made plows and yokes, and taught men righteousness through the products of His peaceful toil.... Later on He was accorded the title of Rabbi because of His profound knowledge of the Scriptures and the Law.

(pp. 53–54)

Cardinal Timothy Dolan, in his book *Doers of the Word*, uses information from current archaeology to explain further that, during Jesus' "hidden" 30 years, St. Joseph

was actually a 'tekton,' an accomplished craftsman. His skills would have been a cross between a designer, an architect, and a construction engineer, not a simple furniture or cabinet maker. Working alongside Joseph, Jesus would have become an artisan in wood, stone, and even metal. Some modern archaeologists *speculate* that with their expertise, Jesus and Joseph may even have worked on the massive construction projects commissioned by Herod the Great, which included a deep-sea harbor, baths, and numerous public buildings.

(p. 14; emphasis added)

We each have much in common with Jesus and the Apostles, who were laborers too. Although the kind of work many of us do differs greatly from the work Jesus and the Apostles did, the point is more about the common ground we have with Jesus for why we work. Pope Francis, in *Laudato Si'*, explains,

Jesus worked with his hands, in daily contact with the matter created by God, to which he gave form by his craftsmanship. It is striking that most of his life was dedicated to this task in a simple life which awakened no admiration at all: 'Is not this the carpenter, the son of Mary?' (*Mk* 6:3). In this way he sanctified human labour and endowed it with a special significance for our development. As Saint John Paul II taught, 'by enduring the toil of work in union with Christ crucified for us, man in a way collaborates with the Son of God for the redemption of humanity.'

(§98)

Working well in the Lord's vineyard is just the point. The world is God's vineyard, and he created us as its caretakers. Why must we work? God has given us the dignity of caring for the world, each other, ourselves, and everything, and we need God to guide us in our work through His grace and the Holy Spirit. While we work, we encounter challenges of various kinds and sizes. Our home-bound isolation during the COVID-19 pandemic revealed the importance, meaning, necessity, and joy of work. This care-taking we do through our work in God's vineyard does not come easily as we participate in society, as we sense the clash of the sacred and the secular.

Society Pressures

As we humans have come to live and work together, we have developed various, necessary, and often successful ways to do that. Allow me to present a very simple way to think about it. We identify shared values and goals. We establish moral expectations and codify ethical frameworks for behavior and decision-making. We create laws to inform each other about and provide structure for what is and is not permitted along with procedures, punishments, and retributions that can be exacted on those who "break" any laws. With all these things, we establish social, industrial, economic, political, technological, and other systems that (individually and in combination) enable us to engage our individual self-interests *and* mutual interests so that individual and shared goals can be realized. Even if religious principles were used to establish any aspect of social systems, what is easy to lose sight of is God.

The finite material world, which God created, is essential to our lives and our work because God created the world for us to live in it. It provides us with the very stuff we need and want so that we can use it as the means to various ends, profane and sacred. The material world is so easily perceivable and usable that we humans in our fallibility very easily (sometimes for some people exclusively) can find it difficult to recognize the world for anything beyond its materiality and utility. After all, we need things of and from the world to help us get through the day in many ways. Social pressures stress values such as wealth, power, honor, and pleasure, all of which are realized through the stuff of this world, including other people as instruments for attaining wealth, power, honor, and pleasure. These are characteristics of what we may call "worldly perfection" (see the *Book of Ecclesiastes* [Chapters 1 and 2] as it points to their vanity). Note, however, that these four things in any form may or may not be bad in and of themselves, depending on what they are, why they are pursued, and how they are pursued. When any of them are pursued for their own sakes above all else, particularly displacing or replacing God, they become sources of sin. Indeed, Bishop Robert Barron explains in *Catholicism: A Journey to the Heart of the Faith* that wealth, power, honor, and pleasure are, according to St. Thomas Aquinas, cardinal sources of sin because humans use them as substitutes for God, as if finite goods are all we need and, as a result, we need more of them to feel better—which amounts to addiction to them. How sad it is to think that other people and God's vineyard itself are but merely means to *our own* ends, to attain some worldly view of perfection. How disappointing it is to think this life we live is only tied to the finite, physical realm. How sinful it is to deny God's role and to not seek in all that we are, say, and do as offerings to God to glorify him. Greatness is a matter of holiness, not worldliness.

In our world, pragmatic matters so often overshadow (if not eclipse or even eliminate) spiritual matters rather than join them all together. This is the clash of the secular and the sacred, as if we can only have one or the other, and the former is seen as superior to the latter. Materiality and spirituality go together—it is a both-and matter, not either-or—because God created everything. God's creation of the material world was not at the exclusion of the spiritual. "It is the spirit that gives life, while the flesh is of no avail" (John 6:63). God gave us His creation in which to live our lives and work in His vineyard, to use the material things and the gifts He's given us to make the world and our lives better for ourselves and each other—and to give Him glory in all that we think, say, and do. He created us in His likeness to enjoy and prosper in His creation for Him, ourselves, and for each other. As Bishop Barron explains in *Catholicism*,

> Even the greatest goods the world can offer—beauty, pleasure, power, esteem, adventure, success—leave the will restless, desiring a still greater good.… [That] even when [the will] is in possession of the highest worldly goods, is a clear indication that the will is ordered to a transcendent value, one that is vaguely sensed but never attained in this life.
>
> (pp. 270–271)

To paraphrase St. Augustine, "Our hearts are restless until they rest in God." As God created the world and needs us to make it fruitful, we know that the materiality and utility of the finite world cannot be all there is. We need each other. *We need God.*

We need God precisely because we are not perfect. When we interact with each other and with the things of the world, we can make mistakes (some worse than others). We all are works in progress, and God knows that. The social, industrial, economic, political, technological, and other systems we create are only as good as we make them, and none are perfect just as we humans are not perfect. The values, goals, morals, ethics, and laws that guide or structure our systems also are only as good as we imperfect humans make them. Yet, with God's grace, Jesus Christ's intercession, and the Holy Spirit's guidance, we can (and often do) make these things and all that we think, say, and do better. (The principles of solidarity and subsidiarity, in addition to the virtues of justice, prudence, temperance, and fortitude, are examples of channels for such divine help.) Social pressures can very well make worldly perfection the goal of life. But we know that our heavenly perfection is the goal, and how we live our lives and work in God's vineyard will determine how well we are suited to attain that goal. So we should think with the end in mind. Work, when done in accord with Christ's teaching and, thereby, the Catholic faith, is as much a means to our personal salvation as anything in life that would help us become holy and worthy of entering Heaven upon our deaths. After all, as St. Benedict says many times in his *Rule*, each of us, particularly those who are responsible for others, will "have to give God an account of all his [or her] decisions and actions" (63:3).

As long as life and work are ordained by God, we owe it to Him to be and do our best with what he has given us, including each other. Successfulness in this life is a function of how well we fulfill God's expectations for us—to uphold His law and apply Jesus' teachings in the Gospels, all of which are echoed throughout the Catholic faith. Social pressures that attempt to keep religion separated from secular endeavors, then, certainly extend into the workplace but have been under scrutiny. As I explained in this book's introduction, religion and spirituality have been all but banned from the workplace, as if the only time and place for practicing one's faith is away from the job—at home and during scheduled religious proceedings in a place of worship. Nevertheless, there is ample evidence from numerous sources over the last two decades, and especially recent years, that that bias has been shifting and is shifting more and more as people realize that their faith is part of who they are and how they live and work.

Spirituality in the Workplace

Spirituality and religion truly always have had a role in the workplace—look at the sacred texts of at least any of the world's major religions and spiritual movements. Patricia Aburdene in *Megatrends 2010* observed, "But the fact remains, most of the world's major religions are somehow linked to business or work life" (p. 69). Even so, certain sociocultural pressures, especially since the Industrial Revolution (perhaps rooted even deeper in the mind and body, spirit and materiality "dualism" advanced by Descartes), have displaced or even banished religion and spirituality from the workplace. Someone is employed to do a job, not to exercise their faith or spiritual practices. In this way, work and faith/spirituality have been separated from each other rather conveniently and, presumably, out of necessity so that the matters of an organization's performance are kept as the sole focal points of everyone's work that contributes to an organization's success. In other words, people should come to work and leave their religion and spirituality at home.

Employees seek greater meaning in their work, and organizations' leaders seek better employee engagement. Such greater meaning and better engagement, as much recent literature shows, is possible (and is being achieved) through integrating spirituality and religion in the workplace. Jeffrey Pfeffer, in his book chapter "Business and the Spirit," shows "there has been growing interest in workplace spirituality and in management practices that permit people to fulfill fundamental values at work" (p. 27). Recall what I said in the Introduction that, as organizations hire employees or admit members of any sort, they hire and admit whole persons who, with their knowledge, skills, abilities, and experiences, also bring their values, faith/spirituality, personality, opinions, wants, needs, cares, worries, and so on.

Organizations with diverse workforces today cannot ignore the intersection of religion and spirituality in the workplace. For practical purposes, there are four particular (but not the only) socio-structural matters that are at play with the intersection of workplace with religion/spirituality. First, the differentiation of religion and spirituality is problematic, as much in the literature (academic and trade) tends to define them as exclusive of one another. But such exclusion belies the fact that, as other literature shows, they truly intersect, as religion definitely is spiritual, but spirituality need not be religious. Separating religion from spirituality, then, seems to be done for argumentative convenience, and the two truly ought to be addressed in tandem, especially when applied in actual organizations.

Second, legal and regulatory provisions in the United States, as part of the *Civil Rights Act of 1964* (and as amended) plus the U.S. Equal Employment Opportunity Commission (at least), guide employers about religions accommodations (inclusive of spiritual practices) and protect employees from discrimination on the basis of religion (inclusive of spiritual orientation). Recent federal rulings through the U.S. Departments of Justice, Education, and Health and Human Services have made the protection of religious liberty in the workplace a major issue to resolve. Very important and recent, the U.S. Department of Labor in May 2020, through a directive by Labor Secretary Eugene Scalia, stated "that agency leaders should incorporate respect for religious freedom into the daily operations of the department." The directive includes ensuring that employees and job applicants receive reasonable religious accommodations, treating equally religious and secular groups seeking funding, respecting all legal religious exemptions (e.g. ministerial exemptions), and enforcing federal laws about anti-religious discrimination (Catholic News Agency, 2020; also see U.S. Department of Labor, 2020).

In the third socio-structural matter, numerous book-length and journal-length examinations of ethics and spiritualty/religion in the workplace demonstrate the greater extent of the benefits of spiritual/religious supportiveness than risks, especially beyond bald performance measures, when it comes to doing the right thing in the right way at the right time for the right people for the right reasons. In short, the integration of religion/spirituality in a workplace results in a positive lift in employee satisfaction and engagement. For the fourth and last socio-structural matter, organizations, through their cultures and business operations, sometimes can be already accommodating of religiousness/ spirituality while others would need adjustments, if they were to do so (large to small, depending on various factors). For example, organizations such as Service*MASTER*, Hobby Lobby, and Chick-Fil-A are well-known examples for their religious foundations and successfulness, but there are many other organizations that are similarly grounded. In addition, many studies give other examples of how religious/spiritual dimensions are instrumental in successful leadership and management, whether or not an organization is overtly religious/spiritually grounded.

One's religiosity or spirituality is, if someone is so inclined, part of who that person is. Whether that person is at home, in a fitness center exercising, in their place of worship or focus, out grocery shopping, or at work, their religious faith or spiritual orientation is very much a matter of who they are and how they live. They employ the precepts of their faith or spirituality in whatever they believe and do because those precepts guide them in living. Even if organizations do not make formal provisions for religion or spirituality in their workplaces, the fact of the matter is that religion and spirituality are already there by virtue of employees who uphold and practice their faiths and spiritualities as vital matters of daily living—they do not offload them like boxes from a truck. That fact strongly suggests at least that organizational leaders who think they can ignore or (worse) suppress religiousness/spirituality among employees are foolish.

More than ample evidence shows, as I have already indicated, that employees whose employers are amenable and accommodating to religion/ spirituality to appropriate degrees (for each organization) are happier in their lives, more satisfied and engaged in their work, stronger contributors to organizational performance and success, and great people to work with and know. The bottom line is that the Catholic faith pertains precisely to Catholics' jobs and careers, and they have every reason to apply the faith in their work as a matter of fulfilling God's will for themselves, coworkers, the organization, and the world.

Challenges to Faith

There will come times when social pressures conflict with our Catholic faith, and there may be times when people with whom we work decry that the Catholic Church is problematic in various ways. In both instances it is vital that we trust the Lord to help us. Psalm 118 (5–9) can be helpful to turn to:

5 In danger I called on the LORD;
the LORD answered me and set me free.
6 The LORD is with me; I am not afraid;
what can mortals do against me?

7 The LORD is with me as my helper;
   I shall look in triumph on my foes.
8 Better to take refuge in the LORD
   than to put one's trust in mortals.
9 Better to take refuge in the LORD
   than to put one's trust in princes.

Very important along with trusting in the Lord to help us is that we, too, must be ready to engage—and do so assertively and calmly *out of love* not defensiveness or anger. As Catholics we have the duty and responsibility to *always* be learning about God and the Catholic faith. No matter your age, you cannot and must not be complacent in what you *think* you know about the Catholic faith and the Catholic Church. You must *truly know* the truths of the faith. So many Catholics do not know the true teaching of the Church as they should. Venerable Archbishop Fulton Sheen once said, "There are not over a hundred people in the United States who hate the Catholic Church. There are millions, however, who hate what they wrongly believe to be the Catholic Church—which is, of course, quite a different thing." Catholics must not be among those in the wrong intellectually, attitudinally, or behaviorally.

You can and must make a difference in helping people, Catholic or not, understand the reality of Catholicism, and if you cannot, you can find out and get back to them with the right information. The area of Catholic apologetics has plenty of enormously informative and instructive sources from which to continue learning. (See this book's Appendix as well as the "References and Selected Sources" list.) Being Catholic means being engaged in the faith daily. At the end of Mass we are charged to "Go in peace, glorifying the Lord by your life" or, alternatively, "Go and announce the Gospel of the Lord." These missions are not platitudes— they are real expectations of Jesus and the Catholic Church because of what we experienced during the Mass. If we do not follow through on these charges, certainly by not continuing to learn about God and the faith as well as not demonstrating our commitment to Jesus' teachings through who we are and what we say and do, we sin, must confess that sin, and must make reparations for that sin, particularly by doing what is expected of us.

If feeling stale, defeated, angry, or weary of the Church and its troubles is the reason for not living the faith and the Gospels, I suggest you pause and rethink things. Although those feelings are real and understandable, you must not leave it at that. Do you similarly disengage and give up on other things in life that are valuable to you, ranging from your family to social issues to your employer? Because you care about them, you engage with them intellectually, emotionally, and behaviorally for the better. You need to do the same with the Catholic faith. Bishop Robert Barron, in his short book, *Letter to a Suffering Church*, which is probably the most poignant and candid piece about the realities of and steps necessary for renewing Catholics and the Catholic Church, says,

> there is simply never a good reason to leave the Church. Never. Good reasons to criticize Church people? Plenty. Legitimate reasons to be angry with corruption, stupidity, careerism, cruelty, greed, and sexual misconduct on the part of leaders of the Church? You bet. But grounds for turning away from the grace of Christ in which eternal life is found? No. Never, under any circumstances.
>
> (pp. 59–60)

Jesus Christ *Himself* (the flesh-and-blood, historical Jesus, the Son of God) established the Catholic Church, with St. Peter as its leader and the Apostles. There is no other Christian church that can claim that fact.

> And so I say to you, you are Peter, and upon this rock I will build my church, and the gates of the netherworld shall not prevail against it. I will give you the keys to the kingdom of heaven. Whatever you bind on earth shall be bound in heaven; and whatever you loose on earth shall be loosed in heaven.
>
> (Matthew 16:18–19)

Notice, too, Jesus did not start His church by name but, very crucially, by mission. (The formal name of the church came later, as we will see.) That mission Christ gave to St. Peter and His Apostles is this:

> Go, therefore, and *make disciples of all nations*, baptizing them in the name of the Father, and of the Son, and of the holy Spirit, teaching them to observe all that I have commanded you. And behold, I am with you always, until the end of the age.
>
> (Matthew 28:19–20; emphasis added)

Further enabling that mission was St. Paul and those whom he ordained to lead the church in nations well beyond Jerusalem. St. Paul, who describes his consultations with St. Peter about his missionary work, reported that Christ Himself called him "so that I might proclaim him to the Gentiles" (Galatians 1:15–24). So, St. Paul is known as "the apostle to the Gentiles." By its Christ-given mission, the church is inherently meant and exists for all peoples and, therefore, is universal—catholic.

The word for this concept of universality in the original Greek (the language used in the original New Testament texts) is *katholikos* (a derivation of *kata hole*), which means "pertaining to the whole" or "universal." The earliest people who believed in Christ, from wherever they hailed, called themselves Christians and members of that one church that was for all, that was *katholikos*. The church, understood as *the* Christian church in its early history, functioned under Jesus' mission for it to be universal as enacted by His Apostles and their ordained apostles (i.e. bishops plus priests and deacons). That church received a formal name based on its mission from Bishop St. Ignatius of Antioch, who, in his *Epistle to Smyrnaeans* in 105 A.D., wrote, "Wherever the bishop appears, let the congregation be there also, just as wherever Christ is, there is the Catholic Church." (Excellent sources about the Church's origin are James Hitchcock's *The History of the Catholic Church*, John Salza's *The Biblical Basis for the Catholic Faith*, Scott Hahn's *Reasons to Believe*, Trent Horn's *Why We're Catholic*, and John Vidmar's *The Catholic Church Through the Ages* [2nd edition].)

All organizations start small. The Catholic Church started with a tiny group of people, comprising Jesus Christ teaching His Apostles and commissioning them to establish His church with St. Peter as the leader. As the Apostles ordained more apostles, they ordained others (particularly bishops but also priests and deacons), and they, in turn, ordained others, and so on over nearly 2,000 years. This approach established "apostolic succession" to ensure ties from Christ's origin of the Church through time, which is one of the four "marks" of the Catholic Church expressed in the *Nicene Creed*. (In addition to being *apostolic*, the Catholic Church is *one* [i.e. being founded by Christ as the one way to God], *holy* [i.e. having been established by God through Christ and enlivened by the Holy Spirit], and *catholic* [i.e. universal for all people and in its wholeness toward salvation]). As organizations grow and gain followers, they become larger, embrace an ever-greater purview, and become more complex to attend to the "business" they must in ways that fulfill the organization's mission. Pope Benedict XVI, in his book *Church Fathers*, explains that Saint Clement, who was the third successor of St. Peter, emphasized the Church's structure in the first century:

> The Church, in fact, is not a place of confusion and anarchy where one [ordained and lay people alike] can do what one likes all the time: each one in this organism, with an articulated structure, exercises his ministry in accordance with the vocation he has received. With regard to community leaders, Clement clearly explains the doctrine of Apostolic succession. The Norms that regulate it derive ultimately from God himself. The Father sent Jesus Christ, who in turn sent the Apostles. They then sent the first heads of communities and established that they would be succeeded by other worthy men. Everything, therefore, was made "in an orderly way, according to the will of God."
>
> (p. 10)

In other words, the organization of the Church has developed over almost two millennia to meet expanding needs and to be able to continuously fulfill its Christ-given mission throughout the world, including to be unified in itself while unifying others in Christ. In this way there is an additional, important reality about the catholicity of the Catholic Church itself, because, as Cardinal Joseph Ratzinger (Pope Benedict XVI) also explains in his *Introduction to Christianity*, "the word 'catholic' expresses the episcopal structure of the Church and the necessity for the unity of all the bishops with one another" (p. 345). The Church is catholic because Christ is ever present in it as the universal source of salvation and because it is on a mission for the whole of the human race. The Catholic Church, with all the documentation available since at least the New Testament writings, has sustained its mission for almost 2,000 years with 266 successors to St. Peter (i.e. popes), where every bishop there ever was (and will be) could plausibly trace back his lineage of ordination to the original Apostles. At least in principle, the Catholic Church not only can make these claims but also substantiate them with documentation.

As Catholics, then, each of us has the duty and responsibility to learn well about the faith and the Church, even questioning what we do not understand; embrace the teaching of the faith that has come down to us directly through the Apostles and their successors; and demonstrate every day in every way that the Catholic faith matters enormously in everything—through actions and words. If the Catholic faith was supposed to be easy, it would be trivial; but the Catholic faith is rich and beautiful in its genius of guidance for living holy lives precisely because life is difficult and we need guidance to fulfill God's will while working in and with His creation, His vineyard. Jesus, through the Holy Spirit, guides the Catholic Church, and we, the Catholic faithful (ordained, professed, and lay people), must trust in Him and, in spite of our imperfections, persevere for our sake and others when times are good and not so good.

Beware of and Conquer Acedia

Again, life is difficult and worth living. Even so, ever have a day where you just did not feel motivated to do much? What about having a string of a few, several, even many days (or weeks or months or years) of lacking motivation to or interest in work? To be sure, multiple causes may be at play, particularly mental health matters that should be properly assessed by and addressed with a mental-health professional, perhaps one who is Catholic. The Desert Fathers, particularly Evagrius Ponticus (345–399), knew well a kind of spirit-sucking malady on our motivation. It is probably one of the most insidious and destructive maladies effected by the devil. It is *acedia* (pronounced "ah-see-dee-uh"), which has also been termed "sloth," "apathy," "despair," and "despondency" that asserts the meaninglessness of life. It also has been often oversimplified as mere depression. The *Catechism* explains:

> The spiritual writers understand by this a form of depression due to lax ascetical practice, decreasing vigilance, carelessness of heart.

'The spirit indeed is willing, but the flesh is weak.' The greater the height, the harder the fall. Painful as discouragement is, it is the reverse of presumption. The humble are not surprised by their distress; it leads them to trust more, to hold fast in constancy.

(§2733).

"Acedia" comes from a Greek word, *akedia*, that means "lack of care." It is that, surpassing laziness or boredom, and far worse. Psalm 143, although it is a prayer for deliverance from enemies bent on killing, can be read as a prayer for deliverance from the ravages of acedia, and you should read and, especially, pray it.

Acedia undermines your spiritual well-being by, as Jean-Charles Nault explains in *The Noonday Devil*, ransacking your very sense of self "that causes [you] to lose the joy of living and paralyzes [your] interior dynamism," as it consists of multiple dimensions at once: "Gloominess, weariness, dejection, sadness, discouragement, disgust with everything, melancholy, boredom, sloth, mediocrity, being 'down' ... All these things are behind our *acedia*, even though, once again, acedia cannot be reduced to any one of these concepts" (p. 107). In this regard, reread the second scriptural spark at the beginning of this chapter and think about the concept of "idleness" as a function of acedia. Moreover, as Kathleen Norris explains in *Acedia and Me*, which is her personal account of combatting the malady, at its worst, acedia not only can "make us unable to care, it takes away our ability to feel bad about that" (p. 45). A kind of deep sadness prevails over all things that would be spiritual goods, and disgust with any activity dominates. Norris pointedly explains acedia as "a kind of spiritual morphine: you know the pain is there, yet can't rouse yourself to give a damn" (p. 3), that it "can deaden what has long been a pleasure" (p. 16) by replacing joy with despair and setting "into motion the endless cycle of self-defeating thoughts" (p. 21). Acedia, if unaddressed, can lead to spiritual (and even physical) death.

Yet there is a cure for acedia, and it is a program that tends to the soul and body. All that God created He said was good, and that divinely inherent goodness in us is precisely that which can eject what acedia, because of human imperfection, has allowed in. R. J. Snell explains in *Acedia and Its Discontents* that

good work wills or approves the goodness of the world, even while developing the world in keeping with its form and rhythm. The slothful, however, (1) abhor the real, (2) have repugnance (sadness) at their own purpose, and (3) are incapable of action in keeping with their own proper good, a profound contradiction and alienation.

(p. 95)

Work, then, is the prescription to cure acedia, because in work and through the means of our work, which God has given us, we find God.

Acedia, as a distraction from the greatness we can become in God's eyes, can be defeated. And it takes time. Indeed, perseverance in our work and all that we are and do is absolutely essential. Remember, too, that greatness comes in all sizes, particularly through little, ordinary things done daily with extraordinary love, as St. Thérèse of Lisieux explained in her "little way," because "God does not see as a mortal, who sees the appearance. The LORD looks into the heart" (1 Samuel 16:7b). Greatness, then, is a matter of holiness, not worldliness. The honor and esteem of others is nice but nothing in God's eyes. Be satisfied doing your work, whatever it may be, the very best you can on behalf of God and His Kingdom.

Evagrius' prescription to conquer acedia, according to Gabriel Bunge in *Despondency*, involves several steps that are not sequential but, rather, recursive, as they must be engaged together and repeated as necessary. His prescription requires endurance, which involves:

- Stability in who and where one is plus what one must do—all the while not giving in to the urge to flee from the situation, as if a "change in scenery" (physical or abstract) will make a difference.
- Confessing one's plight to a spiritual guide, mental-health counselor, or both as a way to obtain support and guidance in the combat.
- Set realistic goals in all tasks and achieve them, using a daily schedule or routine.
- Pray unceasingly for success in all that one does and for freedom from acedia (pp. 96–97).

The self-discipline involved in doing all things well matters, as Snell explains, that

> At all times, it is a matter of putting an end both to idleness and to becoming a 'workaholic' and pursuing working for its own sake, independent of anything else. ... [O]ur ultimate vocation is supernatural rather than natural, rendering our natural vocation 'penultimate' but still good.
>
> (pp. 98, 115)

The supernatural vocation is at odds with society's pressures, which esteems only the natural vocation. Our natural vocation is good because our lives and work on Earth determine (i.e. are the means to) our heavenly inheritance, which means conquering acedia is critical. In another way of thinking, doing the opposite of what acedia dictates would be a key to winning over it.

Integral in Evagrius' prescription for a cure to acedia is prayer—that it be done unceasingly (see 1 Thessalonians 5:17). Someone with acedia who wants to pray must first conquer a lack of willpower to pray, and feeding into this problem is that the spirit of the times sees no point in praying, especially if we think our full calendars leave no room for it.

To be sure, someone cannot merely pray her or his way out of acedia. Evagrius and other spiritual writers about acedia are clear about the cure involving more than just prayer. Prayer must be interwoven throughout one's battle with acedia. Prayer is the lifting up of the heart and mind to (i.e. an act of communication with) God, who wants us to turn to Him in all matters, especially when we are in need.

> Ask and it will be given to you; seek and you will find; knock and the door will be opened to you. For everyone who asks, receives; and the one who seeks, finds; and to the one who knocks, the door will be opened.
>
> (Matthew 7:7–8)

In turn we must listen carefully for and to God so that we are obedient to His guidance during our combat with acedia (and beyond). As Elijah experienced (1 Kings 19:11–12), the Lord may not come in the most-obvious ways but, rather, in the simplest and most-humbling ways, such as a tiny whispering sound instead of a mighty wind, tremendous earthquake, raging fire, or other major event. The Lord's guidance can come through prayer, a spiritual director, a mental-health professional, reading from sacred scripture or spiritual writers, a family member or trusted friend, a situation, or other sources. We must listen and discern carefully.

For myself in my long battle with acedia, I relied on (and still rely on) the stability of a daily routine—home, job, self-care (spiritually, mentally, and physically), and the rest—even as questions and, especially, doubts arose about the meaninglessness of things and how greener pastures seemed to be what I needed. (The devil loves to implant doubt and regret, which can lead to a vortex of negativity!) My persistence and diligence in prayer, study of God and the Catholic faith, work, counseling, and the sacrament of Reconciliation proved very powerful. And it took a long time with discipline, perseverance, faith, and trust in the Lord. It helped to remember that I, like you and everyone else, am a work in progress. In addition, I continue to be watchful for occasions in which acedia may arise, so I can battle it and win.

A sad reality about acedia is that, according to Nicole Roccas in *Time and Despondency*, "the more despondent we become, the more our perspective on prayer is warped.... We forget that it [prayer] is not a 'should' or an 'ought'; it is life itself" (p. 94). To pray, as Bishop Robert Barron has said, make the time to do it, find God as the center of prayer, speak to God honestly as you would a close friend, listen attentively for and to Him, and be silent. Look to the Psalms for inspiration to help successfully conquer acedia, like Psalm 43 (5), which says:

> 5 Why are you downcast, my soul?
>   Why do you groan within me?

Wait for God, for I shall again praise him,
my savior and my God.

For me Psalm 51 (12–14) has been especially important, and it says:

12 A clean heart create for me, God;
   renew within me a steadfast spirit.
13 Do not drive me from before your face,
   nor take from me your holy spirit.
14 Restore to me the gladness of your salvation;
   uphold me with a willing spirit.

Psalm 86 (4–7), too, can be wonderfully instrumental and energizing:

4 Gladden the soul of your servant;
  to you, Lord, I lift up my soul.
5 Lord, you are good and forgiving,
  most merciful to all who call on you.
6 LORD, hear my prayer;
  listen to my cry for help.
7 On the day of my distress I call to you,
  for you will answer me.

The Psalms have something for everyone in every situation and concern in life, and again, Psalm 143 can be a good one to pray to God for vanquishing acedia. In addition to praying for deliverance from acedia's grip as well as going to Mass regularly, you can and should say little prayers along the way every day. Pray even while doing your work so that you may be guided to do your work well and that what you do is both offerings to God and prayers of adoration and thanksgiving for being able to apply God's gifts and creation through the work you do. Especially take some time to pray and offer up your troubles and successes before the Blessed Sacrament in Eucharistic Adoration. The important thing is to pray! You can, as Roccas says, "say prayers without praying, as we can pray without saying prayers" (p. 99), because your resolve to conquer acedia through the *doing and being* of prayerful children of God is part of your seeking stronger relationships with Him. The devil will try anything to keep you from devoting yourself to God. Growth in faith and in love for God is a spiritual, life-and-death combat. If God did not want you to find your way to Him in prayer, you would not win the battle—and you can win. Defeating acedia, then, is defeating the devil. Prayer is life, and your life should be a prayer to God.

The Christian's weapon of prayer, together with perseverance and discipline in living plus the help of mental-health professionals and qualified spiritual guides, can defeat acedia and the devil's demons inciting it, but it takes perseverance and patience. Acedia makes us worry about the past and the future at the expense of the present. Rising to and thriving on challenges builds knowledge, wisdom, and character; avoiding challenges or seeking easy ways out from them perpetuates mediocrity at best. As St. Paul writes, the Lord said to him,

> 'My grace is sufficient for you, for power is made perfect in weakness.' I will rather boast most gladly of my weaknesses, in order that the power of Christ may dwell with me. Therefore, I am content with weaknesses, insults, hardships, persecutions, and constraints, for the sake of Christ; for when I am weak, then I am strong.
>
> (2 Corinthians 12:9–10)

We need *to be* and *to do* in the present so that we live well for God and do His work, fulfill His will, and not ruminate on garbage and waste God's gifts. Stability in our faith-filled lives is a very good thing, which is enabled by the powerful combination of prayer and work.

Conclusion

So, why is work important? Work is good and ordained by God. Work that we do, then, is vital to fulfilling God's mission for us, including overcoming society's obstacles and acedia. We should remember the fact that Christ's work was ordinary like ours *and* done for the glory of God, as He was teaching, praying, feeding, healing, caring, and loving. As Snell explains,

> Recalling that the primary end of work is its subjective dimension, or the development and good of the human person, the universal mandates reveal that each person is called to her subjectivity through the task of good work, with the particular vocation of each (farmer, teacher, banker, homemaker), the living out of the universal creation mandates in a way allowing for the irreducible singularity of each person while simultaneously allowing for the differentiation of vocation needed for society and the common good.
>
> (p. 117)

From the time of my first job delivering papers to today, my motives for work have certainly evolved for the better, especially with a deeper understanding about my role in the Lord's vineyard. For all of us there is so much more at stake for ourselves on earth and, especially, for our souls after death.

> None of us lives for oneself, and no one dies for oneself. For if we live, we live for the Lord, and if we die, we die for the Lord; so then,

whether we live or die, we are the Lord's. For this is why Christ died and came to life, that he might be Lord of both the dead and the living.

(Matthew 14:7–9)

We work because God wants us to do so with the gifts He has given us both spiritually and materially. We can allow ourselves to be defeated by our selfishness and lose ourselves over worthless things professed in the world's view of perfection, or we can seek perfection with God. People cannot serve both God and mammon. Living according to right priorities, with God as primary, directs us to doing the right things with what He has given us according to His law and Jesus' teachings.

Questions for Meditation

- Have you ever thought deeply about Jesus as an ordinary worker? What new ways do you better identify with Jesus so that you may live and work more in His likeness?
- In what ways do you live and, perhaps, express your Catholic faith in your work, in your career, and in dealings with others outside of work and Mass?
- In what ways have you ever experienced symptoms of or felt you have been gripped by acedia? What steps have you or would you take to combat and conquer acedia?

Suggested Activities for Application

- Take an inventory of the types and the degrees of social pressures that have influenced you. Think about their implications on our life, family, career, and other decisions you have made. Consider the kinds of social pressures Jesus faced in his work throughout His life and how you identify with Him. Identify ways you may be able to make improvements, including reviewing any of the sources mentioned in the first chapter, so that why work is important in the Catholic context is clearer to and for you.
- Meditate on and write down any difficulties you have had in working, especially any prolonged apathy, displeasure, avoidance, and other aspects of acedia about work. Consider meeting with a mental-health professional and/or qualified spiritual guide to help you discern what is going on and how you may strengthen yourself.
- Learn more about prayer from sources like the *Catechism* plus books by saints and contemporary Catholic clergy and professed religious who have written about prayer. There are many important aspects of prayer, and you may find the value of varied manners and types of prayer. For example, prayers of adoration and praise, thanksgiving,

supplication and intercession, and contrition are the four prayer types the Catholic Church most prescribes. Vocal prayer (spontaneous or text-based), meditative prayer, and contemplative prayer are important means for communication with God. And the Holy Mass is the greatest prayer of all. Think about how you may enrich your relationship with God (and enhance your work) through better prayer.

3   Who Are We as Workers?

[Jesus said,] 'It was not you who chose me, but I who chose you and appointed you to go and bear fruit that will remain, so that whatever you ask the Father in my name he may give to you.'

(John 15:16)

Above all, let your love for one another be intense, because love covers a multitude of sins. Be hospitable to one another without complaining. As each one has received a gift, use it to serve one another as good stewards of God's varied grace. Whoever preaches, let it be with the words of God; whoever serves, let it be with the strength that God supplies, so that in all things God may be glorified through Jesus Christ, to whom belong glory and dominion forever and ever. Amen.

(1 Peter 4:8–11)

When looking for jobs after graduating from college in December 1986, I found many advertisements (newspapers were the best published sources back then) for positions that I felt were in my field of communication. (And along the way I worked as a full-time, late-shift custodian at an elementary school, in the school district where I worked every summer during high school and college.) As I read hundreds of job descriptions in newspapers, I could see how I fit or did not fit them. For the ones that seemed to be the best fit with my background and interests, I applied. There were always a few for which I firmly believed I was perfect. Out of the many applications for jobs that I submitted, I only obtained a couple of interviews. Although I did not get those jobs, I learned something about how and why the employer wanted to interview me but, in the end, did not want to hire me. If I had thought more about these rejections through the lens of the Catholic faith, I would have discerned that God must have had another assignment for me. As I look back, I think that, for one of those jobs, God gave me a sign. I found that I was one of two finalists, and the reason I did not get the job was that I did not have a master's degree, even though I had a strong internship and the other candidate did not. So, I decided to go back to school to get the advanced degree and strengthen my background.

Thanks be to God, that plan worked well, as I obtained a stronger internship during my graduate studies in writing, then graduated with my master's degree in writing in 1989. Through one of my professors, who was a consultant for a Michigan-based graphic design firm, I applied for and was hired by General Motors to publish owner's manuals. While working at GM, I found that the company would pay for my continued education, which I always wanted to do. So I applied for, pursued, and graduated with my doctorate in communication in 2000. Along the way I left GM to work for a small agency, then become a freelance writer and consultant, then became the director of corporate communications for one of my clients. Having realized my career goals of earning a doctorate, having a solid track record in industry, and having held an executive-level position in communications, with my wife and two young sons, I left industry for academe in 2002 to become a full-time professor, which I always wanted to be but once thought I would only pursue in retirement.

The clarity of God's guidance in my life is most apparent in hindsight. Even though I sometimes recognized some things as signs and followed them, I was not applying the Catholic Faith as overtly as I should have. I believe if I had applied the faith better earlier in my life, I would be a better person, a better Catholic today. But things sometimes take time, and learning is incremental. My work ethic, established through my parents and based on their applications of the Catholic faith, strengthened so that I would pursue things of professional and personal value that would serve me well in my career and life.

So, if we are to consider who we are as workers, we need to look at who we are as Catholics—as religious and spiritual individuals as well as qualified and willing people to do the work we do. We should also examine what we have to offer because of the gifts God has given us through charisms and talents. Then we need to examine how these areas intersect as we work in the Lord's vineyard.

We Are Catholics

At the most basic level, the common currency for what determines someone's eligibility to work and hold a particular job is a combination of knowledge, skills, abilities, and experiences. Other factors like one's character, attitude, reputation, personality, and others also can come into play as needed and allowed by law. Only in very particularly relevant cases might one's religion or spirituality be considered in the hiring process when it specifically matters to the organization and to the job. Even so, as I already described in the preceding chapters, religion/spirituality is most often a nonissue (or forbidden issue) at work. But, also as I explained in the previous chapters, separating one's religion and spirituality from people is impossible. It guides them in all facets of their life and work.

For us Catholics, we are charged to live the faith in every aspect of our lives every day with everyone in everything we think, say, and do. Naturally, then, our work for ourselves, our families, employers, volunteer organizations, parishes, community groups, and so on are literal demonstrations of our Catholic faith. Whether someone is weak or strong in the faith, the point is that the Catholic faith has already provided us with the divine framework for doing good in all that we do—whatever we do for others, no matter who they are, we do unto God. That makes work both a matter of individual *and* community importance, because we work with and for others in our jobs and throughout our careers. Work, then, as Darrell Cosden explains in his book, *A Theology of Work*, and anchors in St. John Paul II's encyclical, *Laborem Exercens*, has true intrinsic value, because work is an *ontological* good (i.e. it is an end in itself), an *instrumental* good (i.e. it is the means through which we obtain the material, economic, and personal stuff we need to live), and a *relational* good (i.e. it provides opportunities for self-expression of one's talents/gifts, charisms, knowledge, skills, abilities, and experiences that contribute to the broader social picture).

Most important to us Catholics, the sacraments guide us in God's call for us to be Good workers in the Lord's vineyard in our lifetimes. Think of the meaning of this chapter's first scriptural spark in this context. Jesus, Himself, gave us the sacraments as means to become holy and to live holy lives for ourselves and others—to give glory to God. Each sacrament gives us particular gifts to guide us in this life, and that naturally includes our jobs and careers. We can understand how those sacraments' gifts enable us to live holy lives by looking at them in the three groups in which they cluster (see *CCC* §1210–1658). Doing so makes understanding and applying them in our lives easier.

The Sacraments of Initiation Are Baptism, Confirmation, and Eucharist

These sacraments together focus on establishing the foundations of living a Christian life by bringing in people to the Catholic faith, realizing and being strengthened by the profoundness of Christ's teaching as the Messiah foretold in the Old Testament as well as His establishing the new covenant of redemption from sin in His blood, and being nourished in soul and body by receiving Christ's Body and Precious Blood. These sacraments of initiation, through sanctifying grace of the Holy Spirit, unify people more closely with Christ, incorporate them into His Church, and enable them to see themselves as integral to and stewards of God's creation, applying the Catholic faith to their daily lives. Words, attitudes, and, especially, actions from Catholics at work, home, and the public square truly must demonstrate the beauty, profundity, and saving power of Christ and His Church, which are remarkably relevant in life and society today and always.

The Sacraments of Healing Are Reconciliation and Anointing of the Sick

These sacraments of healing focus on returning us from our separation from God through our sinfulness, renewing ourselves and our souls for closer union with God through Christ, and embarking on a new fruitful journey toward Heaven in this life by being returned to and living lives of holiness. Pope Francis, in *Gaudete et Exsultate*, explains that

> holiness is experiencing, in union with Christ, the mysteries of his life. It consists in uniting ourselves to the Lord's death and resurrection in a unique and personal way, constantly dying and rising a new with him...[as well as] reproducing in our own lives various aspects of Jesus' earthly life.

(§20)

This point is very consoling as we remember that we are all works in progress and need God's grace through these sacraments. These sacraments renew us in soul, heart, and mind and, most importantly, enable us to be merciful to others as Christ is merciful to us, which is especially important as we engage with many people in a variety of ways any day. Compassion, mercy, and love that emanate from these sacraments of healing must guide us in our daily interactions with others, especially to guard against and even remedy unjust, improper, rash, or other thoughts, feelings, or actions toward others.

The Sacraments of Mission Are Matrimony and Holy Orders

These sacraments focus on building up and serving the community of the People of God. We can think of these sacraments as essentially vocations of marriage that focus on building and living the Catholic faith among all people, from individuals, to families, to parishes, and the world. The first of the two sacraments of mission is the marriage between man and woman who become husband and wife in a family of their own. The second sacrament of mission is the marriage between a man and the Catholic Church, just as Christ's bride is His Church that he entrusted to St. Peter and began through His Apostles. The sacraments of mission mean we are sent to propagate the faith (evangelize) with and for others, meeting and chatting with them "where they are" in their lives about the Catholic faith in all respects, even defending it competently and compassionately when needed.

Charisms (Complementing and Beyond Talents)

When you consider the totality of who you are, from your personality, knowledge, skills, abilities, experiences, and especially the effects of the sacraments, you realize the importance of your uniqueness in God's creation—and the uniqueness of everyone else. Add to these things the gifts from God and charisms from the Holy Spirit. (Revisit the excerpt from Romans [12:3–8] in Chapter 1, as it relates now to this chapter.) Sherry Weddell explains the difference between charisms and talents in her books, *The Catholic Spiritual Gifts Inventory* and *Forming Intentional Disciples.* Gifts from God are those natural talents we each have. They are in-born, perhaps inherited through our genes, and nurtured through our upbringing, experiences, education, and so on. Talents are things we do naturally and primarily for ourselves because we derive much personal enjoyment for being able to do them, and they can be performed for the good of others. Much practice over years is necessary to perfect and make permanent any talents you have. You may even walk away from talents and never employ them again.

Charisms, however, are "gratuitous" gifts from the Holy Spirit that are given through the sacraments, especially those of initiation, and are literally God acting through you. Charisms, Weddell explains in *The Catholic Spiritual Gifts Inventory,* "are focused outward and enable Christians to bear results for the Kingdom of God above and beyond our normal human abilities" (p. 6). Charisms enable you to live in a way that would not make sense if God did not exist. In other words, people in the world around you are broken and have needs, and God's given you charisms through the Holy Spirit to help them. Because humans are imperfect, you will need some time in the practice of any charisms the Holy Spirit has given so you can be as effective with them for others as possible—to perfect them. Charisms are opportunities to live the Catholic faith more fully, to give flesh to the Gospels, as charisms yield joy among others and yourself for doing them. There are no limits to the number of charisms, being supernaturally empowered as they are. Even one's talents may be so empowered. We use our talents and charisms together best for serving the Kingdom of God on Earth.

Through a thorough discernment process focused on identifying your talents and charisms, such as the approach Weddell prescribes, you may discover which ones the Holy Spirit has given you. The basic discernment questions to answer are, "What has God given me for others?" and "What is God doing through me?" Very simply, Weddell presents in *The Catholic Spiritual Gifts Inventory* seven clusters of 24 charisms that the Holy Spirit distributes upon people. Table 3.1 summarizes those charisms individually and by cluster.

Table 3.1 Charisms of the Holy Spirit, according to Sherry Weddell

Charism Clusters and Definitions	*Charisms that "Empower a Christian"*
Pastoral—focus is on nurturing individuals and the community	*Encouragement*—"be an effective channel of God's love"; not a cheer leader but, rather, deeply present for others, primarily by listening, to make matters more bearable *Helps*—"be a channel of God's goodness"; in the background to use one's own or other charisms and talents to enable others to use their charisms and talents *Hospitality*—"be a generous channel of God's love"; understands how God would welcome others who most need His consolation *Mercy*—"be a channel of God's love"; through practical means enables people who are suffering to be restored to dignity, where a person helped feels as though an angel has attended to him or her *Pastoring*—"be an effective channel of God's love"; drawing Christian communities together to administer the faith individually and in small groups
Communication—focus is on communicating truth to change lives	*Evangelism*—"be an effective channel of God's love"; have a burning in their hearts to find out what others' relationship with Jesus is and to help them strengthen it *Prophesy*—"be a channel of divine truth and wisdom"; feel a burning in the heart that Jesus is calling people or others with specific messages *Teaching*—"be a channel of God's truth and wisdom"; learning occurs, not confusion, with openness to teaching methods that work best for others so they reach their "fullest spiritual and personal potential"
Organizational—focus is on structuring an organization or group	*Administration*—"be an effective channel of God's wisdom"; gets things organized through systems, processes, programs, etc., to realize God's goods *Leadership*—"be an agent of God's purposes"; an organizational visionary who sees what is missing or needs attention, then imagines ways to address it *Service*—"be a channel of God's purpose"; very practical approaches by looking at life for what needs to get done and how to do it well *Giving*—"be a cheerful channel of God's provision"; does heavy financial lifting that enables good outcomes, being energized to give and a joy in raising funds
Lifestyle—focus is on a lifestyle and freedom for unusual ministry	*Celibacy*—"be most fulfilled and spiritually fruitful" by always being available to God *Faith*—"be an effective agent of God's purposes"; freely acting on profound trust in God's love, power, and will *Missionary*—"be a channel of God's goodness to others"; one is most alive applying charisms in a culture not one's own to bring about God's goods and goodness *Voluntary poverty*—"be a channel of God's loving presence"; seeks a radical simplicity to enrich others, identifying with the uncertainty of Jesus' life

Charism Clusters and Definitions	Charisms that "Empower a Christian"
Healing—focus is on channeling God's healing and restoration	*Healing*—"be a channel of God's love"; providing physical, emotional, and spiritual healing *Intercessory prayer*—"be an intense prayer" for others; disrupts the devil's work and promotes God's goods and goodness
Understanding—focus is on understanding the ways of God and humanity	*Knowledge*—"be a channel of God's truth"; delves into diligent study and deep learning about God, ourselves, and the universe *Wisdom*—"be a channel of God's goodness"; offers profound insight about situations and approaches to them that enable good decisions *Discernment of spirits*—"be an effective channel of God's wisdom"; immediate knowing or certainty when experiencing the divine and the demonic anywhere anytime
Creative—focus is on creative activity that orders and beautifies	*Craftsmanship*—"be an effective channel of God's goodness to others"; creates something artistic using material from God's creation that others cannot create *Music*—"be a channel of God's creative goodness to others"; someone in the world as a musician, writing and/or performing music for others *Writing*—"be a channel of God's creativity"; using language and/or symbols that, through them, evoke the truth and beauty of human experience and bring glory to God

Talents and charisms reveal us as specialists of all kinds that enable us to be good Catholics at work and elsewhere and all times in God's creation. Notice that the charisms extend and even employ the gifts of the Holy Spirit (i.e. wisdom, knowledge, fortitude [courage], understanding, counsel [right judgment], piety, and fear [awe] of the Lord) as well as the fruits of the Holy Spirit (i.e. charity, generosity, joy, gentleness, peace, faithfulness, patience, modesty, kindness, self-control, goodness, and chastity). Charisms are given for the long term, can be developed, and enable and even magnify other charisms, as we discover, in a sense, that we believe we have found a perfect fit in our lives, maybe feeling a bit like a "holy oddball." Charisms amount to things that someone in the world cannot *not* do, which is divinely inspired as such and certainly not done obsessively or compulsively. Through charisms, the Holy Spirit equips the ones whom God calls. Indeed, charisms are absolutely essential in your life and for others, because they reveal God's reign through what God is doing through you above and beyond your natural abilities to give Him glory. Charisms themselves are seeds of reaching others and revealing Christ, and our employing them bears fruit. In this way, lay Catholics are vital and instrumental to being exemplars of the Church plus building the Church and inspiring engaged disciples of Christ in His Church.

We Work in God's Vineyard

Our work, our toil must sow Jesus' word of life and to, then, reap the harvest in joy. This point is at the heart of this chapter's second spiritual spark from St. Peter. Here it seems the point is discerning your calling, your *vocation* for working in the Lord's vineyard (see the text in Chapter 1 about discernment, in the section Lay Authors' Writings) so you can make the most of your charisms, talents, knowledge, skills, abilities, and experiences. This concept of vocation is about much more than what one does for one's self. Vocation is an interior calling to which one responds enthusiastically and authentically to muster his or her strengths, talents, charisms, energies, knowledge, skills, abilities, experiences, and so on to engage creatively and competently in service and leadership with and for others. A vocation can encompass one or more jobs one holds in a career, but a vocation truly is more than any job. Consider these pithy maxims: *Live to work; work to live. Do what you love; love what you do.* These truly get to the heart of who we are as workers: We are collaborators with God in taking care of His creation (1 Corinthians 3:9). Yet we still seek what God would have us do and be for Him.

We can understand and discern our vocations in the vineyard. Michael Novak, in his book *Business as a Calling*, explains four characteristics of a calling. First, no one's calling is like that for someone else—each person's calling is unique. God wants us to be and to apply our talents, charisms, and all that we are in particular ways that glorify His creation. Second, one's calling hinges on preconditions that transcend desire and talent by fitting our knowledge, skills, abilities and thriving on love for the drudgery and the joy, the struggles and the triumphs that come from work. Third, the consistent and constant renewal of energy that comes from working in our vocation, even in the face of burdens, dreads, or roadblocks. Perseverance and persistence are key, especially "to test the spirits to see whether they belong to God" (1 John 4: 1). And fourth, one's calling is difficult to discover without thoughtful discernment, prayer, patience, and trust in God. Listening carefully for and to God, not to society's pressures, is vital, like it was for Elijah, when he was listening for God on a high mountain, but did not hear Him in violent wind, an earthquake, or a fire but, rather, in a "light silent sound," like a tiny whisper (1 Kings 19:11–13). "For I know well the plans I have in mind for you—oracle of the LORD—plans for your welfare and not for woe, so as to give you a future of hope" (Jeremiah 29:11).

Working in a vineyard, the ultimate product is wine. That product is not possible without a wide range of people doing a great variety of things. (Think of the business of winemaking as it is today compared to Jesus' time.) And when the wine is finally ready, it is bottled and provided for people to enjoy, including the vineyard workers. Wine is very important throughout the Bible and in the Holy Mass. Being a worker in the Lord's vineyard, then, is divine, natural, and essential, especially when we find our vocation, giving us meaning through meaningful labor.

"Vineyard" in this sense is more metaphorical than literal; yet the meaning is the same—the fruits of our labor are for the glory of God, that we, too, may offer up our work and products as well as enjoy them ourselves because our vocation is from God, to Whom we owe so much.

Learning and mastering all the facets of any job takes time, often years. Sometimes we find we work in jobs that are unfulfilling and not for us. We also have times when we "screw up" to varying degrees, some simpler than others, and other times we endure adversity of greater or lesser effects through factors within or beyond our control. Through it all we must trust in God that such experiences are to prepare us for something better to serve Him and others in His vineyard. Remember,

> we even boast of our afflictions, knowing that affliction produces endurance, and endurance, proven character, and proven character, hope, and hope does not disappoint, because the love of God has been poured out into our hearts through the holy Spirit that has been given to us.
>
> (Romans 5:3–5)

Through our work we develop our talents, charisms, virtues, and personal character plus our knowledge, skills, abilities, and experiences, so we can further contribute to the welfare of others and God's vineyard. Through it all our Catholicity should guide us as we build a record of accomplishment, reputation, and network of relationships that demonstrate who we are, what we can do, and how we can add value to others' lives, including organizations of any sort.

There is a fire in each of us to make great contributions for others, ourselves, and God in His creation. Remembering that God, through the talents, charisms, abilities, and all the rest He gave us, ignited that fire is often difficult to do. This point is central to integrating the Catholic faith and our work. As James Nolan explains in his book, *Doing the Right Thing at Work*, "our religious faith and traditions are highly relevant to what we do at work, as in all aspects of life" (p. 20). Doing good and being good matter all the time. The ultimate objective for this life is to get into Heaven and be in God's presence for eternity, even if that means a stop in purgatory first. We can only achieve this objective by trusting that the Catholic faith is the path to holiness and eternal life. While work is an ontological, instrumental, and relational good, the everyday tasks, duties, and challenges require us to do what is right and best always.

Indeed, the Catholic faith in all its respects (as this book presents simply) provides us with a highly reasonable and greatly applicable framework to live well according to God's Law and Christ's teaching. It is society and secular values—all, I daresay, at the devil's bidding—that foment questions, doubts, and dismissal of the Church and its teaching and relevance. Personal pride and ego serve to rationalize errantly that the Catholic faith has no or little place in our work or life. We must engage in spiritual combat because we know better! We workers in the Lord's vineyard, in all our roles and capacities (leaders and followers alike, masters and apprentices), are entrusted to do for others and for God the right things in the right ways at the right times for the right reasons. As Jesus taught us, "[Y]our kingdom come, your will be done, on earth as in heaven" (Matthew 6:10). All of this requires us to actively know, embrace, and apply the moral principles and ethical precepts that pertain to and emanate from the Gospels on which the Catholic Church and its teachings, through the intercession of the Holy Spirit, are built and have withstood for two millennia.

Conclusion

So, who are we as workers? We are collaborators with God in His creation, using the very "stuff" of His creation as the means to care for it and provide for all those living in it.

> For thus says the LORD,
> The creator of the heavens,
> who is God,
> The designer and maker of the earth
> who established it,
> Not as an empty waste did he create it,
> but designing it to be lived in. (Isaiah 45:18)

We are workers willing and able to do what God calls us to do and to be, even if that means enduring jobs or tasks that are not what we want. Trusting in the Lord that He has a plan, a kind of path for our vocation is key. In fact, surrendering to God through Christ and with the Holy Spirit is what matters in making sure we recognize the value of, employ the virtues of, and reap the fruit from our talents, charisms, knowledge, skills, abilities, experiences, and all the rest so that our contributions, no matter how large or small, simple or complex, give glory to God.

Filled with God's spirit and graces, we become more thoroughly ourselves and can better fulfill our purpose in His vineyard, effectively using God's gifts to us as gifts to others. Everything we are and do as workers in God's vineyard matters, and separating our Catholic faith from any aspect of our lives, especially our careers, is nonsense. Pope St. John Paul II said definitively in *Christifideles Laici*:

> There cannot be two parallel lives in their [lay people as members of the Church and citizens of human society] existence: on the one hand, the so-called "spiritual" life, with its values and demands; and on the other, the so-called "secular" life, that is, life in a family, at work, in social relationships, in the responsibilities of public life and in culture. The branch, engrafted to the vine which is Christ, bears

its fruit in every sphere of existence and activity. In fact, every area of the lay faithful's lives, as different as they are, enters into the plan of God, who desires that these very areas be the "places in time" where the love of Christ is revealed and realized for both the glory of the Father and service of others. Every activity, every situation, every precise responsibility—as, for example, skill and solidarity in work, love and dedication in the family and the education of children, service to society and public life and the promotion of truth in the area of culture—are the occasions ordained by Providence for a "continuous exercise of faith, hope and charity.

(§59)

We are called as Catholics to live the faith and grow in it always through prayer, study, and the work we do that applies what we derive through prayer and from study of God and the faith. Living the Catholic faith through our words and actions is the surest way to demonstrate its relevance and importance to ourselves individually and to society. We become more fully human and ourselves through realizing the vocation God has for us in His vineyard and, then, taking the steps to fulfill that vocation, which we practice for God, ourselves, and for others. The steps toward a vocation may well be small at first or maybe even unsavory at times, but with trust in God and His need for us to be and to do as He wills in his vineyard, progress would be made and fruit from our labor would be bountiful.

Questions for Meditation

- Do you see your work as your vocation? In what ways have you or have you not considered your work your vocation?
- What in your career path, from your earliest days seeking a job to today, do you see God's hand guiding you to make you who you are today? How does that make you feel?
- What among your talents, charisms, knowledge, skills, abilities, experiences, personality, character, and so on is most instrumental in your life that enables you to be who you are and to collaborate with God in his vineyard? What do you learn about yourself and your relationship with God?

Suggested Activities for Application

- Think of the sacraments, even explore them in more detail in the *Catechism*. For each sacrament, identify particular ways it can be and has been instrumental in your work and your career, pointing to particular examples or situations where that instrumentality was especially prominent.

- Reflect on yourself as a Catholic worker, identify your strengths and weaknesses, then consider opportunities to make your strengths stronger and to minimize or eliminate your weaknesses. Also consider what interior and exterior threats may impair your self-improvement. See what kind of plan action you can make in your self-improvement.
- Discover your charisms and explore them (and your talents and temperament/personality) deeply by contacting the Catherine of Siena Institute (www.siena.org) to identify when and where *The Called and Gifted Workshop* may be scheduled near you.

4   How May We Have Faithful Careers?

> There are different kinds of spiritual gifts but the same Spirit; there are different forms of service but the same Lord; there are different workings but the same God who produces all of them in everyone. To each individual the manifestation of the Spirit is given for some benefit.... But one and the same Spirit produces all of these, distributing them individually to each person as he wishes.
>
> (1 Corinthians 12:4–7,11)

> And whatever you do, in word or in deed, do everything in the name of the Lord Jesus, giving thanks to God the Father through him.
>
> (Colossians 3:17)

For all the jobs I ever held, the interviews were always both exciting and scary. They were exciting because there was a very real possibility I would actually get the job I wanted, and I could envision the kinds of short- and long-term benefits I would have from the job. The interviews were scary because I did not know the person or people with whom I was discussing my qualifications and abilities for adding value to the businesses, and I realized the reality of the actual work experience could be worse than, better than, or the same as what I expected. Of course, in comparison to all the career-oriented job interviews I have ever had in my life, the interviews for my earliest jobs were the simplest. For those early jobs, I just needed to be genuinely eager, capable, and committed to doing the work, and someone I knew (sometimes someone who already worked there) could vouch for me and my character. Even so, with all I knew about myself, how was I going to do all they wanted me to do? Job applications and interviews, whether they lead to the job you want or not, are the necessary steps in moving into and through your career. In this way, the work we do to get any job is a job in itself, but the real work is in maintaining your career wherever it leads you.

When thinking about how it is that you may have a faithful career, it seems that the factors in getting jobs you want, doing well in them, and keeping them for as long as you wish until you want or need to move on are all that matters. But thinking about what the preceding chapters have covered (and those that follow), having a faithful career is so much more than tending to the mere mechanics and the secular or materialistic matters behind our motivations to work in any capacity and keep working until we retire, win a big lottery jackpot, or be born into eternal life. *Gaudium et Spes* from Vatican II explains:

> This split between the faith which many profess and their daily lives deserves to be counted among the more serious errors of our age. The Christian who neglects his temporal duties, neglects his duties toward his neighbor and even God, and jeopardizes his eternal salvation.

> (§43)

Work, as we have seen, has an inherent spiritual value that is inextricably intertwined with it because God wants us to contribute to His creation in the ways that each of us can that are unique to each of us, are supportive to each other and all of us together, and give glory to God.

The question of how we can have faithful careers is best answered by examining at least two dimensions to it. The first is the collection of selected ways and means for working and living that the Catholic faith upholds—for knowing and improving who we are and what we contribute as Catholics, extending topics from the previous chapter. The second dimension is what could be called "recipes" that are integral in the Catholic faith—guides for all that we do always, especially in our work, that help us maintain right priorities.

Selected Ways and Means for Catholic Working and Living

Socrates is credited with the maxim, "Know thyself," which is important and at the heart of being a Good person. Sometimes each of us needs a little more help to get to know ourselves better, which is especially possible through the sacrament of Reconciliation, and then make lasting improvements in ourselves. A lot of money is spent—estimated by John LaRosa at Marketdata Enterprises in 2019 to be $11 billion in the United States—on self-improvement (also known as "self-help" and "self-care") material, including sources like books/audiobooks, CDs/DVDs, infomercials, speakers, workshops, conferences, seminars/webinars, retreats, personal coaching, internet courses, mobile apps, and more, that is meant to inspire positive physical, mental, spiritual, or financial change for people. Through Jesus Christ, the saints, and the Catholic Church, we already have access to myriad means for self-improvement—to become saints ourselves. Among those ways and means already available to us Catholics through our faith (and there are far more than will be covered here), several are worth highlighting because of their special application to faithful careers.

Prayer

In any relationship communication is vital—and not just any communication but communication that is meaningful, honest, loving, trusting, engaging, and so on. It is no different with our relationship with God. Prayer, as we already saw in Chapter 2, is sincere and active communication between us and God, where listening is as important (if not more) as speaking. Prayer is the lifting of the heart, mind, and soul to God and, in this way, is not a mere technique but, rather, a matter of personal engagement with God. Prayer is paradoxical in that at times it is wonderful and rich but other times challenging and impoverished. So faithfulness and perseverance in prayer are necessary because of the importance of our relationship with God, and prayer must be done daily with God, just as we communicate with the people in our lives at home, at work, and elsewhere. In this regard, Fr. Jacques Philippe's book, *Time for God,* is a wonderful catalyst for better prayer.

Fr. Philippe explains that events in life, ranging from painfully disruptive ones to joyously welcome ones, deserve special spiritual attention through prayer, especially as matters of faith, hope, and love. Times of trial are important times to lean on God, because they are opportunities to obtain God's graces according to His will. The reasons for the way things go may not be clear immediately, but trust there will be revelations to lead you on your way to fulfill God's will. Prayer, as an act of faith, expresses belief in God, His love, and the value of spending time with Him to build and nourish the relationship in times that are good, bad, and in between. Prayer as an act of hope is a natural way to express trust in God and await the growth of His graces. Prayer as an act of love is a sincere and true expression of seeking God to do His will and give him yourself because of love for Him. If you have faith in, hope with, and love of God, you can trust He will be present and take care of you.

Openness to prayer leaves openness to God in our life. Profound revelations are not the focus of prayer but, rather, incremental, persistent graces that make a big difference over time. Prayers of supplication and intercession call upon God and, perhaps, a selected saint, for help in specific circumstances that are especially important to us and present a great trial in life. Prayers of adoration and praise give to God our deepest love for Him as God, our Heavenly Father, as well as express our humility before His awesomeness, He who gave us life and the cosmos. Prayers of contrition express our personal sorrow for sin, plead for God's forgiveness and mercy, and offer repentance from our sinfulness, while we also beg for guidance and perseverance to not sin again. And prayers of thanksgiving express our deepest appreciation for what God has done and given us in specific ways and in all ways, including offering Him the fruits of our labors because we know He enabled us to do good and do well in His vineyard.

During the course of any day, you can pray any time, such as when doing dishes, pulling weeds from a garden, taking a walk, commuting to work (even if it is to another room in your home), preparing a project, lying wakeful in bed, and so on. And do not worry about distractions (they happen); just catch yourself and return your focus back to God with your prayers. Prayer can be spontaneous from the heart *at any time* or nurtured from any source, such as the Bible, the Lord's Prayer, the Rosary, the Stations of the Cross, or a book of Catholic prayers. Making special time in Eucharistic Adoration before the Blessed Sacrament would be especially good and fruitful. The Mass is the greatest prayer, which is why it is so important to attend Mass on Sundays and on Holy Days. Fr. Romano Guardini, in his book, *The Art of Praying*, stresses the importance of preparation for prayer that involves the "recollectedness" of being composed and concentrating in the now, being present in the act of praying, being unified with the very reason for prayer that is rooted in God, and being awakened interiorly with the fullness of God and His grace. If the mere thought to pray occurs (seemingly out of nowhere), consider it God wanting to "touch base" with you, so take the opportunity to chat even if it is just briefly to say, "I love you, Lord."

We need prayer greatly because this world needs the peace that surpasses understanding that only God can give—and we must be God's means to securing that peace in the world. Prayer enables us to find peace, receive God's graces, and discern what He would have us do and be, especially at work when beginning the day, going into a meeting, toiling on a task alone or a group project, handling a conflict, or other situations, including the trip to and from the place where we work. With God as the center of our prayer, He is the center of our lives, which is as it should be. God at the center of our life puts all else in its proper place.

Charisms and Talents

Who we are, what we can do, and how we actualize ourselves are a reflection of God's and the Holy Spirit's gifts to be and to do in the Lord's vineyard. As we saw in Chapter 3, talents and charisms are not to be undervalued, and they are to be perfected. We should take stock of your own charisms, talents, knowledge, skills, abilities, and experiences and discern how we can best engage them. God loves us for all that we are and can do, and we must make returns on those divine investments in our vineyard work for God, including giving thanksgiving and praise to Him. At Mass the Offertory is the faithful presentation of "the work of human hands" in the forms of bread and wine as well as monetary donations to the church. Edward Sri, in *A Biblical Walk Through the Mass*, explains that these offerings are sacrifices from individual toil in our quest for God—"giving of our entire lives to God in the offering of bread and wine" (p. 87).

In our daily lives, charisms and talents reveal the both-and of faith and works as the very "stuff" of daily life, not just something for Sundays or special occasions. James (2:26) asserts that "For just as a body without a spirit is dead, so also faith without works is dead." Good works done in the faith matter everywhere and for everyone in the Lord's vineyard, and they come with certain graces. In a way, St. Francis de Sales reveals in his *Introduction to the Devout Life* that the fruits or "rewards" of talents and charisms are "tokens of the joys of everlasting life, occasionally granted to [people] in order to kindle in them a desire for the fullness of joy which is only to be found in Paradise" (p. 90).

Love

We can best understand love as willing the good of others as others, as Bishop Robert Barron has explained in his works. When we approach our lives, work, and relationships through such love (*agape* love) we make connections with the greater good and truth that each person seeks and shares for one's self, for others, and, most important, for God. When we think of love in this sense, love is a kind of communion between people that is perfect. Pope Benedict XVI, in *Caritas in Veritate*, explains that love "is the principle not only of micro-relationships (with friends, family members, or within small groups), but also of macro-relationships (social, economic, and political ones)" (§2). Love requires good judgment. It may mean saying no and disappointing someone. It may mean giving harsh truth about something when that truth is not what someone wants to hear (sometimes called "tough love"). It may also mean celebrating success or mourning loss.

Love is the supreme guide in life, particularly when working and leading others. The following familiar quote from 1 Corinthians applies just as much at work as anywhere:

> Love is patient, love is kind. It is not jealous, [love] is not pompous, it is not inflated, it is not rude, it does not seek its own interests, it is not quick-tempered, it does not brood over injury, it does not rejoice over wrongdoing but rejoices with the truth. It bears all things, believes all things, hopes all things, endures all things. Love never fails. If there are prophecies, they will be brought to nothing; if tongues, they will cease; if knowledge, it will be brought to nothing.
>
> (13:4–8)

When in any situation, especially at work, reflecting on this passage can help diffuse and diminish ill will we may feel as well as inspire and intensify joy. Love is everything and is of God and is God. When we act or speak with love, we reveal God to others.

Humility

Perhaps the greatest illustration of true humility is the parable of the Pharisee and the tax collector in the Gospel of Luke (18:9–14). The Pharisee went to the forefront of the temple area and prayed in thanksgiving that he was not in the least like all other sinners, especially the tax collector; whereas, the tax collector distanced himself from the inner temple area and mortified himself and prayed to God for mercy for his sinfulness. Jesus concludes, "'I tell you, the latter went home justified, not the former; for everyone who exalts himself will be humbled, and the one who humbles himself will be exalted.'" Jesus gives the same admonition in Luke's Gospel (14:7–11) in the parable about assuming a position of honor at a wedding feast when it is not appropriate until the host offers the higher position. Humility, then, benefits from detachment to worldly things, is absent of great pride or overblown ambition, and enables one to turn effortlessly to God, especially for His mercy.

As we saw in Chapter 2, social pressures for wealth, power, honor, and pleasure abound and command that we acquiesce to and adopt them as the essential matters in life, not God. The devil inspires the social pressures for worldly things, but humility fueled by genuine love of God and detachment from the world wins. In spite of our egos, we are not as important as we like to think we are. Why? Self-importance is a function of the mortal sin of pride. Christ is our salvation not because of egoistic self-assertion but, rather, the humility of self-giving. So for us, too, humility is a means for God's graces to reach us as we live by self-giving (service), not self-assertion (pride). Self-giving is the heart of humility and Christ-like. St. Francis de Sales explains,

> the highest point of humility consists in not merely acknowledging one's abjection, but in taking pleasure therein, not from any want of breadth or courage, but *to give the more glory to God's Divine Majesty, and to esteem one's neighbor highly than one's self.*
>
> (p. 102; emphasis added)

St. Antony of Egypt (lived 251–356), known as one of the greatest among the "desert fathers" of the early Christian Church and the "father of monks," said of a vision he had, "I saw the devil's snares set all over the earth, and I groaned and said, 'What can pass through them?' I heard a voice saying, 'Humility'" (Ward, 2003, p. 148).

When people say they are "humbled" by some recognition or award for something they did or achieved, they must be wary of harboring inordinate ambition or great pride, which itself is a mortal sin. True humility is the realization that all good things that one possesses or achieves are from God (see *CCC* §2559). Any recognition of or honor for good or exceptional work we do is not for us personally but, rather, for God, who works through us and deserves our praise and thanksgiving for doing well and revealing His glory because of His graces. St. Benedict says in his *Rule* we must "desire to attain speedily that exaltation in heaven to which we climb by the humility of this present life...[but we descend away from heaven] by exaltation [in worldly matters]" (4:5–7). With humility we know how God has blessed us through His gifts and why we are responsible for perfecting them to both give Him glory (i.e. praise and thanksgiving) and use the fruits of our labor for others, ourselves, and His creation.

Obedience

Following directions and submitting to imperatives are examples of obedience. But note that obedience is not meant to be blind. The word, "obedience," has as its root word that Latin word, "*audire*," which means "to hear, to listen." This fact makes obedience much more dialogic than monologic. That is, obedience entails people engaged together in achieving understanding and cooperation, even seeking knowledge and wisdom, making efforts to resolve differences and dissent to discern the most fitting response that would be enacted. Indeed, as St. Benedict says in his *Rule*, "Obedience is a blessing to be shown by all, not only to the abbot but also to one another as brothers, since we know that it is by this way of obedience that we go to God" (71:1–2). As it is in human relations and human activity, things are often ordered in some way with rules and norms, and such ordering can imply or depend on some kind of hierarchical relationships among people so that leaders and followers work together to achieve particular ends. Remember what Jesus said about his true family in the Gospel of Matthew (12:46–50) that, "'For whoever does the will of my heavenly Father is my brother, and sister, and mother.'" Remember, too, Christ's own obedience to suffer and die on the Cross to fulfill the Father's will for the salvation of the world.

Embedded in obedience is humility, as understanding, agreement with, deference to, or cooperation in the matter at hand leads to requisite and appropriate action under God's guidance and in tune with His will. St. Benedict in his *Rule* explains, "With the ready step of obedience, they follow the voice of authority in their actions" (5:8). The *Catechism* explains obedience is due to divine law by submission to God for the sake of salvation, legitimate civil authority whom God allowed for the sake of the common good and social order, to parents, and to the word of God through the Catholic faith. St. Paul says in his letter to Titus (3:1–2), "Remind them to be under the control of magistrates and authorities, to be obedient, to be open to every good enterprise. They are to slander no one, to be peaceable, considerate, exercising all graciousness toward everyone." In terms of a faithful career, then, obedience requires us to recognize God's primacy in all things, and humility tempers our response to situations and outcomes that we prefer or not prefer. God's will, then, comes to us from leaders as well as from peers, from those senior to us as well as those who are junior, as "the Lord often reveals what is better to the younger" (St. Benedict, *Rule*, 3:3). (How we apply our talents, charisms, knowledge, skills, abilities, and experiences comes into play here.) God's will, then, should be discerned carefully, even prayerfully, so that understanding that will, being obedient to that will, and being accountable for any outcomes may garner the graces that are most beneficial to our salvation and the salvation of others.

Discretion

Self-control is so important in so many ways. St. Francis de Sales acknowledges that "This miserable life is but the road to a blessed life; do not let us fall out by the way one with another; let us go on with the company of our brethren gently, peacefully, and kindly" (p. 109). Discretion, then, is at the heart of self-control, as we exercise suppression of anger, restraint in speech, and avoidance of rash judgment, among other urges. Instrumental in discretion is reason, humility, and love, because these graces allow us to recognize the triggers that "set off" visceral responses (negative *and* positive) and, then, direct energies to manage them interiorly as well as exterritorialy for others involved.

In a very real sense, discretion is a kind of reflection on the statement, "What would Jesus do?" Even if someone were to come to you enraged about something, responding in kind would be counterproductive and, essentially, un-Christian. Calmness and assertiveness borne out of reason, humility, and love can effect good results, whether administering reproof, correction, or punishment as much as administering praise, kudos, and pardon. Mercy and compassion are very important in discretion too. Plus, silence can be a very good thing, especially as it is essential in prayer and to listening well. As St. Benedict in his *Rule* says in application of Psalm 39, "there are times when good words are to be left unsaid out of esteem for silence. For all the more reasons, then, should evil speech be curbed so that punishment for sin may be avoided" (6:2).

A fair degree of familiarity with and practice in conflict management, especially tempered by Catholic teachings and self-awareness, also can go a long way to managing yourself and managing others. Indeed, St. Francis de Sales reminds us that, in discretion, it is best to remember that "Humility makes our lives acceptable to God, meekness makes us acceptable to men" (p. 108). Additionally, he emphasizes that we need to "exercise gentleness" with ourselves, "never growing irritated with one's self or one's imperfections" in the face of knowing that we despise our faults and need to refrain from becoming angry or despondent over them (p. 111). A guiding light in and for discretion is to see Jesus Christ in others. Overall, keeping focus on God and knowing that His gifts for us to labor well in His vineyard will help greatly in exercising discretion wisely.

Discipline

Discipline is keeping focus on the things that most matter among the myriad things that inundate our senses and sensibilities, to uphold a great degree of self-control and fastidiousness in all pursuits. Discipline is developed through practical training about our work and our day-to-day duties, responsibilities, and expectations in our professions. Discipline also comes through the rules and norms we follow in our daily lives, which in all respects both enable and lead us in every experience. The Catholic faith provides us with a rich, durable, and usable framework for fostering personal discipline that begins directly from Jesus Christ and His teachings, and Jesus' church has grown and developed through the Holy Spirit's intercession.

Just as the Bible is a coauthorship between God and the writers of the books of the Bible, the Catholic Church is a collaboration between God and humans over nearly two millennia whom God has employed—even in the face of their fallibility, imperfections, and occasional failures—to establish the church Christ Himself entrusted to St. Peter and his successors. As Venerable Archbishop Fulton Sheen once said on his television show *Life is Worth Living*, "If our Lord wanted a perfect church, He would have put His angels in charge." The Catholic Church itself, despite the failings of its leaders at times, has prevailed against diabolical assaults from within and without for almost 2,000 years as a model of diligence and discipline focused on bringing everyone to Christ. Very important for us, the canonized saints (including those who are "venerable" and "blessed" but not yet canonized) are models of discipline plus diligence and determination—all for the Kingdom of God that we can experience on Earth through the Holy Mass and, particularly, in all we do and are as workers in the Lord's vineyard.

Patience and Perseverance

The old term of "stick-to-itiveness" comes easily to mind. On the one hand, we must be patient to obtain the outcome of any effort, and on the other hand, we must persevere in our efforts to obtain the desired outcome. In this way patience and perseverance go together necessarily. Patience is the willingness to wait for something in modest anticipation or suffering, and perseverance is the exertion of energies and the application of available means to sustain momentum toward some end. So, "sticking to it" means one endures all the adversity and blessings that come along with achieving some end—one exercises patience and perseverance.

"Have no anxiety at all, but in everything, by prayer and petition, with thanksgiving, make your requests known to God. Then the peace of God that surpasses all understanding will guard your hearts and minds in Christ Jesus" (Philippians 4:6–7).

The world's ways today promote instant gratification as a virtue; they foster people who are so often restless, impatient, and nearly incapable of perseverance. People want what they want when they want it, and sometimes if they cannot get it, they can become angry or spiteful or both, none of which is the least bit charitable. In some cases a need truly must be met immediately, such as for medical emergencies, mechanical failure, organizational crisis, or other situations for which time is of the essence in obtaining a proper resolution. Much more often, however, time is not of the essence and, indeed, sufficient time must pass because there are many things that must be done before an outcome is realized. During that time people can become weary and disengage their energies that are so necessary in maintaining progress.

Weariness is a weakness the devil uses to separate us from God and keep us from maintaining a strong relationship with Him (Acedia can apply here too.). It is important to remember the parable of the persistent woman in Luke's Gospel (18:1–8) who did not grow weary, because the parable illustrates the importance of being persistent and in persevering. She asked a judge to grant her a request for a just decision in a conflict she had with someone, and he turned her down multiple times. She persisted, she persevered, she was patient, and he eventually granted her the request for a just decision. Jesus, in summing up the parable, says, "Will not God then secure the rights of his chosen ones who call out to him day and night? Will he be slow to answer them?" Similarly, Jesus' parable of the sower (Luke 8:4–15; also Matthew 13:18–23) teaches the importance of perseverance (and its very close cousin persistence). As Matthew (13:18–23) recounts the parable, we must not be like the seed that falls on rocky ground, which "hears the word and receives it at once with joy. But he has no root and lasts only for a time. When some tribulation or persecution comes because of the word, he immediately falls away." Jesus explains in Luke's gospel (8:15) that "for the seed that fell on rich soil, they are the ones who, when they have heard the word, embrace it with a generous and good heart, and bear fruit through perseverance."

The necessary catalysts behind patience and perseverance are charity and discipline, for without those catalysts, progress is lost and outcomes are lost as well. Humility, too, matters in exercising patience and perseverance, which, as St. Benedict in his *Rule* explains, the "heart quietly embraces suffering and endures it without weakening or seeking escape" (7:35–36). As much as they are essential to the work we do, patience and perseverance are essential to the faith and in prayer too. Fundamentally, our souls yearn to be with God, but being bound on Earth means the best we can do is to "stick to" our labor in the Lord's vineyard until He calls us home to Him. St. Augustine said in his *Confessions*, "You stir man to take pleasure in praising you, because you have made us for yourself, and our heart is restless until it rests in you" (I.i[1]). We seek the coming of God's Kingdom and must not "abandon [our] earthly tasks; faithful to [our] master, [we] fulfill them with uprightness, patience, and love" (*CCC*, §2046).

As part of a faithful career, while we plan then execute projects, two main dimensions are apparent. First, we are mindful of God's centrality in our lives to labor well in His vineyard and the obligation to acknowledge Him in our labor. And if there are struggles or suffering, as St. Benedict says, "What is not possible to us by nature, let us ask the Lord to supply by the help of his grace" ("Prologue," v. 41). Second, we know how important it is to effectively marshal and manage the God-given resources of people, money, facilities, material, and time. Amidst our daily duties for prayer *and* for work, we have numerous commitments to fulfill for God, others, and ourselves. St. Francis de Sales, in his *Introduction to the Devout Life*, emphasizes, "Live ever, then, ye resolutions, which have an eternity of your own in God's Mercy, live ever in me, and may I never forsake you" (p. 238). Patience and perseverance are invaluable, and through it all we must trust in God to guide us in our labor to bear fruit in His vineyard in due time.

Witness

You are a Catholic. Whether at home, at play, at work, or at wherever, you keep and live the faith. You are an example of the Catholic faith to others in all that you are, say, and do. You are a witness to the Catholic faith every day in every way. Sometimes, by carefully observing people, you can tell certain things about them and often be correct. You profess the faith through your life through your words and actions, even if they are not specifically and obviously expressions of Catholicism. Identifying and being identified as a Catholic is a wonderful thing, because we live in the joy of the Gospels, and that joy is reflected in how we live our lives, so do not be shy about it. Being Catholic forms every aspect of our lives, and it should. In a twist on a spiritual song with which you may be familiar, "They'll know we are Catholics by our joy!" Doing ordinary things with extraordinary love, as St. Thérèse of Lisieux prescribes in her "little way," fits this idea well. Pray before meals in restaurants and elsewhere. Make a habit to pray 10, 15, or more minutes a day in solitude. Wear a Miraculous Medal or a Scapular and understand why they are important. Carry a Rosary and use it. Apply the principles covered in this book and other Catholic sources overtly. Apply principles of the faith always in your day, as you probably already have been and can do so more overtly, deeply, and joyfully.

If times come that we must testify to the faith to any degree, we must do so confidently and without equivocation. A quick prayer to the Holy

Spirit asking for guidance would be most appropriate. The *Nicene Creed* and the *Apostles' Creed* are excellent places to start, because they summarize the Catholic faith and direct you to the essential things. Very much like we are supposed to in our careers, where we must stay up to date in our fields of expertise, continuing to learn about the Catholic faith will give the knowledge, confidence, and capabilities to represent Catholicism well. Simple, nonthreatening, and even impromptu conversations with people are best, with the natural ebb and flow of topics, energy, curiosity, and humor. Be yourself! In the workplace, as we have already seen, religion and spirituality are already points of interest and matters of people's daily lives, although the comfort levels people have with discussing religion and spirituality (when and where) may vary. In this context, hospitality as well as compassion, trust, and love become very important and appropriate. Even if such conversations never happen, exemplifying the Catholic faith by your life is natural and expected. No matter how you do it, living the faith well and with love shows you are living by right priorities.

Recipes for Right Priorities

Purpose drives action. When we know what it is that we or others want or need, we devise an approach to meet that want or need, whether it is as simple as going to the grocery store to get food for the week or as complex as developing a plan to communicate a major organizational change. As Catholics, all that we do in life is not just for the sake of living but, rather, to live holy lives so that we become saints and enter God's glory upon our death. As Thomas Merton explains in his book *Life and Holiness,*

> A saint, then, seeks not his own glory but the glory of God. And in order that God may be glorified in all things, the saint wishes himself to be nothing but a pure instrument of the divine will. He wants himself to be simply a window through which God's mercy shines on the world. And for this he strives to be holy.
>
> (p. 24)

Holiness is possible! You can be a saint!

Indeed, placing God at the center of our lives enables all the rest of who we are and what we do to follow. The Catholic faith provides us with "recipes" for actualizing our purpose in this life. Yes, the Bible presents these recipes, which means they pertain to other Christian religions too, and that is good. Nevertheless, for us Catholics, given the Biblical basis of the Catholic Church and its teachings over two millennia, these recipes have a richer tradition and deeper connections between us and God through Christ and His church. For example, the recipes all underscore the supreme importance of having right priorities—that God must be the center of our lives, and from that point, all else follows (see Matthew 6:33). Additionally, the Holy Sacraments tie to all of these recipes and are instrumental for us to receive God's graces. We humans want and need order in life. Among the many recipes or guides available so we order our lives along right priorities, several are especially worth highlighting because of their particular pertinence to faithful careers.

The Ten Commandments

Known as "the law" given by God through Moses (Exodus 20:2–17; also Deuteronomy 5:6–7, 11–12, 16–21), the Ten Commandments define the relationship between people and God. Although the Ten Command-ments were established for the ancient Israelites, they applied in Jesus' time. "'Do not think that I have come to abolish the law or the prophets. I have come not to abolish but to fulfill" (Matthew 5:17). Moreover, the Ten Commandments apply to us today and for always: "It is easier for heaven and earth to pass away than for the smallest part of a letter of the law to become invalid" (Luke 16:17). The commandments are as follows, as presented in the *Catechism of the Catholic Church* (§2052–2082):

1 I am the LORD your god: you shall not have strange gods before me.
2 You shall not take the name of the LORD your God in vain.
3 Remember to keep holy the LORD's Day.
4 Honor your father and your mother.
5 You shall not kill.
6 You shall not commit adultery.
7 You shall not steal.
8 You shall not bear false witness against your neighbor.
9 You shall not covet your neighbor's wife.
10 You shall not covet your neighbor's goods.

Christ taught that observing the commandments was required of all His followers, indeed for all of humanity. Christ further extended the "Old Law" by adding the "New Law" of the covenant He established:

One of the scribes…asked him, 'Which is the first of all the command-ments?' Jesus replied, 'The first is this: "Hear, O Israel! The Lord our God is Lord alone! You shall love the Lord your God with all your heart, with all your soul, with all your mind, and with all your strength." The second is this: "You shall love your neighbor as yourself." There is no other commandment greater than these'" (Mark 12:28–31).

The commandments express the fundamental duties people have to-ward God and for others. They apply in all human activity, and to break one is to break the whole of the law. Love is the fulfillment of all the commandments (Romans 13:10). Within the context of a faithful career, it is easy to imagine how any of the commandments apply and, most important, guide us in what we think, say, and do through our jobs and our labor. And always doing what we do out of love means we are working and living right priorities and abiding by the commandments well.

Lord's Prayer

Jesus, in his teaching about prayer to his disciples (Matthew 6:9–13, which is the version closest to the one used in the Mass; also see Luke 11:2–4), provides not only a taxonomy of content for proper prayer to God, but he also provides us with the ultimate prayer for us to pray to God. Notice how the beginning of the Lord's Prayer echoes the first two of the Ten Commandments. Of course every line in the prayer matters, and in that prayer, at least two lines (taken from the Roman Missal) are especially noteworthy for faithful careers. The first is "thy kingdom come, thy will be done, on earth as it is in heaven." Here we see the importance of living for God's kingdom, including our work in it; discerning God's will and using his gifts (talents and charisms) in the fulfillment of that will in all that we think, say, and do; and recognizing that, even with free will, obedience to His law and His will is paramount.

The second line in the prayer worth highlighting is "forgive us our trespasses as we forgive those who trespass against us." Here we see the importance of mercy and that we, *ourselves*, are responsible for whether or not we attain salvation and enter God's presence in Heaven. As Luke (6:36–38) reports that Jesus said to his disciples:

> Be merciful, just as your Father is merciful. Stop judging and you will not be judged. Stop condemning and you will not be condemned. Forgive and you will be forgiven. Give and gifts will be given to you; a good measure, packed together, shaken down, and overflowing, will be poured into your lap. For the measure with which you measure will in return be measured out to you.

The *Confiteor* that we recite early in the Mass is an especially important recognition of our own responsibility for our own salvation or condemnation upon our deaths because of sins we have committed. For a faithful career, imagine at least the results for eternal life because of personal transgressions in not making the most of God's gifts and not being merciful and forgiving of others. Psalm 146 (3–4) says it well:

> 3 Put no trust in princes,
>   in children of Adam powerless to save.
> 4 Who breathing his last, returns to the earth;
>   that day all his planning comes to nothing.

Repenting from sin, partaking of the sacrament of Reconciliation, and making reparations for the sins committed at home, at work, and anywhere at anytime can lead to redemption and right reordering toward God.

The Beatitudes

To be happy in this life that God has given us in His creation, there are particular things we need to remember that further extend the Ten Commandments and support the *Lord's Prayer*. The commandments and, now, the beatitudes (Matthew 5:3–10), are not restrictions on freedom—they are the foundations of freedom. Simplistic minds see freedom (and by extension liberty) as doing whatever one wants, but that actually is chaos and leads to anarchy and moral depravity, as someone is a slave to one's own desires, whims, and perversions without regard to anyone or anything but one's self. Think of freedom this way: Anyone without prior experience can produce sounds from a musical instrument or, in another example, start saying random words in another language. But in each case the person is incapable of the freedom of playing the instrument well (even innovatively) or speaking the language well (even fluently) until that person has understood the design, nature, and rules that govern their use and mastered them. Not having rules, parameters, laws engenders chaos not freedom, because anything goes.

The law and beatitudes compose a framework for achieving freedom joyously for and with others because the exercise of freedom is directed toward God. Freedom is, as the *Compendium: Catechism of the Catholic Church* (§363–366) explains, the God-given power to act or not, including choosing good or evil. Freedom attains perfection when it is directed toward God. Bishop Robert Barron, in his book *Catholicism*, gives a wonderful treatment of the beatitudes. He divides them into two groups, "positive formulations" and "negative prescriptions," then explains how they affect certain graces or outcomes. Table 4.1 summarizes Bishop Barron's explanation.

When considering the beatitudes in the context of faithful careers, it is not difficult to see how any one of them can be encountered and acted upon to realize the grace or outcome so that both you and others are secure in the pathway to salvation. Remember Jesus' teaching in the Gospel of Matthew (25:45–46) about the judgment of nations: "'...what you did not do for one of these least ones, you did not do for me.' And these will go off to eternal punishment, but the righteous to eternal life." Indeed, the beatitudes themselves are a compass for the mind, heart, and soul to always find their way to and through the path of holiness without straying through sin. The important key here is to see Christ in everyone.

Table 4.1 The beatitudes, as summarized by Bishop Robert Barron

Group	Beatitude	Grace Realized or Outcome
Positive formulations (*set right priorities that orders one's soul and being toward pleasing God*)	Blessed are they who hunger and thirst for righteousness, for they will be satisfied.	Ultimate concern is righteousness
	Blessed are the merciful, for they will be shown mercy.	Centrality of divine love
	Blessed are the clean of heart, for they will see God.	Focused on God
	Blessed are the peacemakers, for they will be called children of God.	Unifier of all things and people under God
Negative prescriptions (*corrections for the things that St. Thomas Aquinas says we use [i.e. abuse, allow addiction] to fill the space we don't fill with God; see Chapter 2*)	Blessed are the poor in spirit, for theirs is the Kingdom of Heaven.	Corrects for addiction to wealth
	Blessed are they who mourn, for they will be comforted.	Corrects for addiction to pleasure
	Blessed are the meek, for they will inherit the land.	Corrects for addiction to power
	Blessed are they who are persecuted for the sake of righteousness, for theirs is the kingdom of heaven.	Corrects for addictive attachment to honor/ approval

The Virtues

Any virtue is "the habitual and firm disposition" to always do what is good (*Compendium*, §377–388). Virtues enable us to channel our passions intellectually and willfully so that our words and actions are in concert with reason and faith under God's law. Virtues can and should be perfected by repeated application of them in situations where they pertain. There are two categories of virtues. The first category is the "cardinal" virtues, which means they are the primary or principal virtues for human conduct. The four cardinal virtues are *prudence* (i.e. the cause of other cardinal virtues; a moral sensibility about good and evil, especially in the service of the love of God), *justice* (i.e. give to each person what is his/ her due), *temperance* (i.e. disciplining of the desires to serve the demand to love), and *fortitude* (i.e. courage; constancy in the pursuit of the good). Integral with the cardinal virtues is the second category of "theological" virtues, which have God as their origin, motive, and object.

The theological virtues are especially important in enabling us "to live in a relationship with the Trinity" and provide "the energizing force of the Christian's moral activity" under the cardinal virtues. The three theological virtues are *faith* (i.e. belief in God and what He has revealed; belief in

Church teaching and willingness to apply that teaching), *hope* (i.e. anticipation for eternity in God's presence in Heaven and in His guidance in this life), and *charity* (i.e. love of God above all things and of our neighbors as ourselves; it is the foundation of all other virtues). Among the virtues, seeing how they directly apply as vital matters in faithful careers is easy, for every circumstance will call upon one or more of them, especially for assessing situations; identifying possible approaches to those situations; evaluating which alternative approach is best; making good decisions about what to do, how to do it, when to do it, and for whom to do it; enacting the plan of action; and measuring effectiveness, making adjustments, and obtaining lessons learned.

Works of Mercy

When we think of mercy, we think of giving love and compassion to someone or some group of people who is experiencing some form of rejection and is in need of unconditional love. The best example of mercy is the story of the prodigal son in the Gospel of Luke (15:11–32). To perform any work of mercy is to enact God's love most directly and for the benefit of another. There are two categories of works of mercy, and they are shown in Table 4.2. The "corporal" works of mercy focus on the goods necessary for the health of the body. The "spiritual" works of mercy focus on the goods necessary for the health of the soul.

As the body is the temple of the soul, good care for both is necessary, and sometimes a little extra help is needed through one or another work of mercy so that the whole person is well. The works of mercy, then, are ways that we channel God's love for humanity for those in need of it by whatever means are available. On the job, spiritual works of mercy for bearing wrongs patiently and forgiving injuries can prove challenging, but they must be done and done with love. Employees also can offer corporal works to help colleagues and others in need. During the COVID-19 pandemic, works of mercy abounded in various ways, particularly corporal works of mercy but also spiritual works through local parishes. As much as the works of mercy can be applied by individuals to individuals

Table 4.2 The corporal and spiritual works of mercy

Corporal	Spiritual
• Feed the hungry	• Admonish sinners
• Give drink to the thirsty	• Instruct the ignorant
• Clothe the naked	• Counsel the doubtful
• Visit and ransom captives	• Comfort the sorrowful
• Shelter the homeless	• Bear wrongs patiently
• Visit the sick	• Forgive all injuries
• Bury the dead	• Pray for the living and the dead

or groups of people, they also can be applied by organizations to individuals and groups of people. That is, for-profit, nonprofit, governmental, nongovernmental, and other types of organizations can and do perform works of mercy, most often as philanthropic efforts focused on particular social and cultural issues.

The Precepts of the Church

The Catholic Church reminds us that we have certain basic or minimum duties as Catholics, and they pertain to our whole lives. These duties are called "precepts," and there are five of them (*CCC* §2041–2043):

- Attend Mass on Sundays and holy days as well as rest from servile labor.
- Confess sins at least once a year.
- Receive Holy Communion at least during the Easter season.
- Fast and abstain from meat on days the Church says.
- Provide for the Church's needs according to one's abilities.

The purpose of these precepts is to make sure that we always engage in our relationship with God in ourselves, with others, and with the Catholic Church through its liturgy and sacraments. We must remember to *not* merely give lip service to the Commandments, Christ's teachings, and the Catholic faith while "[hating] discipline and cast[ing] [God's] words behind [us]" (Psalm 5:16–17). The first precept is foundational because the Mass, as *Sacrosanctum Concilium* from Vatican II says, "is the summit toward which the activity of the Church is directed" (§10), and proper praise of God enables us to more and more embrace and live God's graces. We engage through prayer and the moral effort that results in the growth in our love of God and of others. Notice, then, that the precepts actually benefit us all the time, at home, at work, at play, at prayer, and everywhere. The precepts give us ties back to all the other facets of the Catholic faith that are necessary in strengthening and living it in all that we are and do for others, ourselves, and, primarily, for God as we labor and live in His vineyard.

Conclusion

So, how may we have faithful careers? Surrender ourselves to God. Conversion from sinfulness to the Catholic faith in every facet of our lives is essential—the saints did it, and so must we. Jesus said to his disciples,

> If anyone wishes to come after me, he must deny himself and take up his cross daily and follow me. For whoever wishes to save his life will lose it, but whoever loses his life for my sake will save it.
>
> (Luke 9:23–24)

It can be easy to lose sight of this principle in our secular lives—that the relevance and application of the Catholic faith as the spiritual counterpart to all we are and do. Thomas Merton, in his book, *Life and Holiness,* explains,

> The spiritual life is not a life of quiet withdrawal, a hothouse of growth of artificial ascetic practices beyond the reach of people living ordinary lives. It is in the ordinary duties and labors of life that the Christian can and should develop his spiritual union with God.
>
> (p. x)

People often say someone "has their whole life ahead of them," as if human lifespan is very long. We only have this life God gave us to work well and profitably in His vineyard according to His will, then He will call us home, if and only if we are worthy to be in His eternal glory. Psalm 90 (9–10, 12) points out that

> 9 Our life ebbs away under your wrath;
>   our years end like a sigh.
> 10 Seventy is the sum of our years,
>   or eighty, if we are strong;
>   Most of them are toil and sorrow;
>   they pass quickly, and we are gone. ...
> 12 Teach us to count our days aright,
>   that we may gain wisdom of heart.

So, we Catholics have the opportunity and the responsibility in our short faith-filled careers to, as the Pontifical Council for Justice and Peace's *Compendium of the Social Doctrine of the Church* explains,

> strengthen [our] spiritual and moral lives, becoming ever more competent in carrying out [our] social duties. A deepening of interior motivations and the acquisition of a style appropriate for [our] work in the social and political spheres are the results of a dynamic and ongoing formation directed above all to the attainment of harmony between life, in all its complexity, and faith.... Bringing faith and life together requires following the path judiciously indicated by the characteristic elements of Christian living: the Word of God as a reference point; the liturgical celebration of the Christian Mystery; personal prayer; the authentic experience of Church enhanced by the particular formational services of discerning spiritual guides; the exercise of the social virtues and a persevering commitment to cultural and professional formation.
>
> (§546)

Questions for Meditation

• How would you characterize your career up to this point in your life as a "faithful career"? Where do you see yourself doing well, and where do you see yourself needing to improve? How would you proceed to improve yourself in light of these revelations?

• Among the "ways and means" for Catholic living, which one(s) stood out to you and why? What does that observation suggest to you on how to have a more faithful career?

• Similarly, among the "recipes" for right priorities, which one(s) stood out to you and why? How do you think those recipes (and any of the others) can be especially instrumental to you having a more faithful career?

Suggested Activities for Application

• Look back at this chapter's spiritual sparks and meditate on them by reading them slowly several times. After each reading, note what stands out from them and why you think that is so. From what this chapter has presented, think about whether and how these scriptural excerpts can help direct you, through the Holy Spirit, to a better faith-filled career and life.

• Using each of the "recipes for right priorities," brainstorm at least one example from your career or from your imagination that fits each part of each recipe. (For the Lord's Prayer, you should use the whole prayer, not just the two lines featured in the text.) Identify what you did/would do, why it is/is not consistent with the faith, and how you could improve. Think deeply about each example and its lessons for you as a Catholic seeking a more faithful career and life.

• Reread the closing quote from the Pontifical Council for Justice and Peace. How do you see yourself fitting in or not fitting in or somewhat fitting into what it says lay Catholics must do. Note what factors in your present job help and hinder your living the faith at and through your work. Also note what factors in the future of your career you think will help you or hinder you to having a properly faithful career. Consider what would you need to do in the near, medium, and long term to realize a more faith-filled career and life.

5 Where May We Find Help?

Therefore, encourage one another and build one another up, as indeed you do. We ask you, brothers, to respect those who are laboring among you and who are over you in the Lord and who admonish you, and to show esteem for them with special love on account of their work. Be at peace among yourselves. We urge you, brothers, admonish the idle, cheer the fainthearted, support the weak, be patient with all. See that no one returns evil for evil; rather, always seek what is good [both] for each other and for all.

(1 Thessalonians 5:11–15)

Brothers and sisters: I, a prisoner for the Lord, urge you to live in a manner worthy of the call you have received, with all humility and gentleness, with patience, bearing with one another through love, striving to preserve the unity of the spirit through the bond of peace: one body and one Spirit, as you were also called to the one hope of your call; one Lord, one faith, one baptism; one God and Father of all, who is over all and through all and in all.

(Ephesians 4:1–6)

My first full-time, career-oriented job after graduating with my bachelor's and master's degrees was with General Motors. I was a publisher for vehicle owner's manuals, where my principal job was to have owner's manuals for particular lines of GM vehicles printed and distributed to assembly factories. My job required me to be sufficiently knowledgeable about the publication process, particularly for books, and I was but not in everything. Plus there was GM's way for publishing the information for vehicle owners. For the first nine months I was in a constant up-hill learning curve about many things, particularly the company. I worked with two other very experienced and collegial colleagues who had the same kind of job I did, and they were very helpful. I sought help and got it from my boss, my two colleagues, others with whom I needed guidance for parts of my job about the business of the company, and many other sources. I received a promotion after about two years and moved upstream in the publication process to be more of a technical writer and editor of owner-focused information than a publisher of it. My knowledge of the company, its products, its services, its processes and policies, and people in certain areas of the company enabled me to find and acquire other positions in the company that helped me advance in my career.

For any job that I started after the one I held, with increasing levels of responsibility and authority, it was a new beginning. I had all the "right stuff" for the job, but there was always so much more to learn. And that is the key: There is always more to learn—the learning curve is real. After all, how many times in our jobs have we been befuddled by something and needed another source—a manual, a memo or report, a person, a graphic or illustration, a dataset, a *something*—to figure it out and move on with some confidence? We humans are fallible, no matter how intelligent, experienced, skilled, capable, or otherwise self-reliant. It is great to have answers on the top of our minds, tips of our tongues, tips of our fingers, but no matter how much we think we have prepared, the likelihood of our needing some kind of help is good. And that is okay!

We are all life-long learners, and that characteristic is especially important as Catholics. With a faith that is nearly 2,000 years old and has the depth and breadth of profound truths, teachings, and traditions, we should expect that the Catholic faith and the Catholic Church have so much to offer us to truly help us live lives of holiness and have faithful careers. Finding the sources that can best help us when we need it—to guide us in our understanding and application of the Catholic faith in our lives and careers—is very doable and can be very fruitful. The first places to which to turn are the Catholic Church itself, then we turn to Catholic clergy and religious, publications, unceasing prayer to God, and fellow Catholics.

Catholic Church

We can live holy lives! Society tells us holiness does not matter at all or matter as much as wealth, power, pleasure, and honor. The society's pressures perpetuate that lie, propagated among people like the devil tried to tempt Jesus in the desert (Luke 4:1–4; Matthew 4:1–11). Holiness is a prominent principle in and of the Catholic faith. Thomas Merton, in *Life and Holiness*, explains that

> A 'holy' person is one who is sanctified by the presence and actions of God in him. He is 'holy' because he lives so deeply immersed in the life, the faith, and the charity of the 'holy Church' that she manifests her sanctity in and through him.

> (p. 16)

Everything that the Catholic Church teaches points to holiness as the ultimate objective we must seek, for in seeking it daily we become more like Christ and better prepared for eternal life with God. In *Lumen Gentium*, which is the central document to come from the Vatican II, explains in its fifth chapter that holiness, founded on genuine love of others as others, is a universal call among all baptized Christians no matter their state of life. Holiness "is unceasingly manifested, and must be manifested, in the fruits of grace which the Spirit produces in the faithful; it is expressed in many ways in individuals, who in their walk of life, tend toward the perfection of charity, thus causing the edification of others" §39). Our time on Earth may seem long, but it is nothing compared to eternity. As long as we realize the temporal limit we face is the only, fleeting timeframe in which we have to make the most of God's investment in us (*tempus fugit, memento mori*), we must take steps through the Catholic faith to repent from our sinfulness, convert to be true and active followers of Christ, and submit to God's will and graces.

The saints are great examples of holiness, and they came from many varied backgrounds. Many were consecrated religious and many were not, living ordinary lives much like us in their times in history. In every case they were sinners like us. Events in their lives, either sudden or gradual, perhaps in their youth or later in their lives, profoundly affected them to recognize the truth of their calling to holiness and pursuing it heroically through the Catholic faith into which they were baptized. The saints are heroic examples of holiness to us, and that heroism is not meant to throw us off by sounding lofty but, rather, inspire us precisely because of their ordinary lives, conversion, and submission to living in and through Christ in order to fulfill God's will. The stories of the saints' lives are truly amazing to read and well worth the investment in reading them. Saints across the ages, including our own age, are great models of how the Catholic faith can and must be instrumental in our lives to be fruitful workers in the Lord's vineyard.

The saints, just like us, had essential sources to guide them. Similar to going on a journey for a vacation, for which you would likely collect information, maps, example itinerary, and other material to help you, your journey of faith needs authoritative and credible source material. The Catholic Church always has had that material available to everyone, beginning with the ultimate source of Jesus Christ Himself. There are three core sources for the Catholic faith, which are explained in the *Catechism*. The first source is the *Deposit of the Faith*, which includes Sacred Scripture and Tradition. These contents have been in existence and handed down through the ages from the Apostles. Sacred Scripture in the Bible presents the entire salvation story of and for humanity, climaxing with Jesus' resurrection and ascension plus the beginning of evangelization about his being the Salvation of the world, and it is essential to guiding us in our lives. Sacred Tradition, beginning principally from the Gospels and applying the other books, subsumes theological, disciplinary, liturgical, or devotional forms of the faith that make real the lessons about God and living holy lives gained through the ages thanks to the Holy Spirit's intercession in the life of the Catholic Church. The second source for the Catholic faith is the *Magisterium*. This source concerns the living teaching authority of the Catholic Church that serves the Word of God. The Magisterium is particularly lively through the pope and his infallibility in matters of the faith and morals, draws authority through the Deposit of the Faith, and formulates divinely revealed principles for belief. The third source for the Catholic faith is *Dogma*, which is divinely revealed truth that, through the Church's infallible teaching authority (Magisterium), is formally established as solemn decrees within the Church's ordinary, universal teaching. All dogma is infallibly defined. A formal rejection of dogma, then, constitutes heresy. Stemming from dogma is *Doctrine*, which is belief or teaching that the Catholic Church officially approves through the pope himself or the college of bishops—all while exercising the authentic teaching through the Magisterium. Doctrine enables our faith journey by giving the tenets of the faith in precise and usable ways. Only the pope, benefitting from any counsel of the Roman Curia and College of Cardinals, can promulgate dogma and doctrine. From these core sources around which the Catholic faith revolves, the Catholic Church creates a wide variety of discourse to evangelize, explain, and otherwise instruct and engage people around the world in the Catholic faith and the Catholic Church's enactment of the Word of God in their lives.

Remember that the foundation of the Catholic Church is not human in origin—it is divine, having been made manifest by God through Jesus with and for humans for their salvation, beginning with the Apostles. The Deposit of the Faith, Dogma, and Doctrine, although made manifest through humans (yes, those humans have been and are principally men, and women have long held and continue to hold vital roles and made and continue to make vital contributions), were given to all people by God for human application. The Deposit of the Faith and Dogma are infallible. Along with Doctrines of the Church, Principles of the Faith (i.e. Canon Law) on particular matters may not be infallible, but they are based on the infallible teachings of the Church and are authoritative because of the influence of the Magisterium. To the extent that any Principles or Doctrines are not infallible, they could undergo change, such as changes that were made through Vatican II for the Mass. (For a useful summary of dogma and doctrine, see Jimmy Akin's explanation online at jimmyakin.com.) The Catholic Church needs and thrives on the interaction of diverse people who individually and collectively seek God's Kingdom and work to fulfill His will.

As imperfect as we humans have been, are, and shall always be (after all, how we exercise free will can move us closer to or further away from God), we must trust in God, Jesus, and the Holy Spirit to always guide the Church and its people (clergy, consecrated religious, and laity alike) through the good and the bad of life. Although divine in its origin, the

Catholic Church is still imperfect as an institution because of its humanity. Over its history the Catholic Church has seen and, because of free will, its people have contributed to a share of corruption. But through it all the Church has remained and risen above it by the grace of God, sought forgiveness and reconciled for its faults and failings, and shall always prevail as a divine institution in which we must participate to fulfill God's will and live lives of holiness for each other and Him. In a way, then, the Church's longevity is evidence for how good overcomes evil and remains resilient and relevant through all time. To guide us all (clergy, consecrated religious, and laity alike) in both living out and improving the Church, we must continue to adhere to the Church's teachings until it is clear from God (i.e. per Magisterial infallibility in matters of the faith) that any change is best and must be instituted.

Catholic Clergy and Religious

Just like anyone in any profession, priests and deacons (i.e. clergy who have received the sacrament of Holy Orders) as well as nuns, monks, and other consecrated religious (i.e. people who freely enter, in response to Christ's call to perfection, and take vows of poverty, chastity, obedience, and perhaps other vows) have undergone much formation and preparation for their vocation in the Catholic Church, plus they actively continue their formation for the rest of their lives. Catholic clergy and religious are near us always wherever we go, as they are in parishes, monasteries, or houses/communities. Generally speaking, they have as their mission to bring God through Christ to others. They are our guides in the faith that we need and God has given us.

Clergy and religious people are wonderful sources of and for the Catholic faith. You can meet with your parish priest or with a nun, for example, to obtain guidance about an important matter in your life or to have questions about Catholicism answered. If the clergy or religious member with whom you meet thinks someone else or some sources may be additionally helpful, he or she will say so and direct you to how to obtain that help. Remember, too, that the sacrament of Reconciliation also is a grace-filled way to both obtain from Jesus Christ, through the person of the priest, absolution for your sins and gain insights into ways to improve yourself. Being the works in progress that we are, reception of the Eucharist also obtains many other graces and should be received frequently, especially after receiving the sacrament of Reconciliation.

Vocations in religious life generally fall into two broad categories. The first or "primary" category (also referred to as "order") is that of ordained priests and deacons. The second category is that of consecrated or professed people of religious communities (e.g. Benedictines, Carmelites, Dominicans, Franciscans, Passionists, Salesians, and others) who are themselves part of the Catholic Church and its mission, and they take vows that pertain to their specific spiritual organization and rule for living. Lay Catholics who would like greater integration of the Catholic faith in their lives and a stronger relationship with God and Jesus Christ may consider joining a lay order of Catholic religious organizations (also referred to as "secular," "third," or "tertiary" order) such as those just listed for the consecrated and professed vocation. As lay members of a religious order, they make solemn promises but not vows. For example, Jesuits operate the Pope's Worldwide Prayer Network (formerly called Apostleship of Prayer), which is open to ordained, consecrated, and lay members and is very good in its own way. Opus Dei, founded in 1928 by St. Josemaría Escrivá, is a Catholic spiritual organization that is focused on evangelizing the Church by enabling Christians to sanctify all aspects of ordinary life, especially work. Working in the spirit of Christ, Opus Dei members bring God's love to others in what they do by doing it competently, ethically, and with the love of God when serving others.

Members of lay orders make solemn promises they endeavor to fulfill to the extent they can in their states of life, which do not have the same weight as vows and consequences for breaking them. Each religious organization (alternatively referred to as an "order") has its own "charism," and you may discern to which one you are called. Ample information is available online, including data about where they are near you so you can talk with them and learn more. I am an Oblate of the Order of St. Benedict (Obl.OSB) and a member of the community at St. Bede Abbey in Peru, Illinois. I have found the Benedictine charism works very well for me in many ways to discover and maintain my proper relationship toward God, my family, civil society, and religious living. Benedictines exercise the values of peace, listening, fidelity to God, prayer, work, stability, humility, obedience, hospitality, discipline, patience, charity, justice, and moderation. It has been a wonderful way to deepen my relationship with God and Jesus Christ through applying St. Benedict's *Rule* in my life, particularly by integrating prayer and work, which manifests Christ's presence in society. Balancing the spiritual and the temporal is not easy, as secular forces abound, but being in a lay order definitely helps put things in their proper order.

Publications (Print and Digital)

The vast array of publications for and about the Catholic faith provides us with additional and usable insights, advice, instruction, knowledge, and wisdom for our quest for faithful careers and faith-filled lives. The first chapter of this book presented a solid collection of good publications authored by Catholic religious leaders, spiritual guides, scholars, businesspeople, and others. These works offer us a wonderful array of inspiring and practical sources to help us on our ways to become saints.

The Bible is available in printed and digital forms. Whether printed or digital, publications of all kinds covering all topics imaginable about Catholicity are well worth the investment of time reading them, reflecting on them, and applying them. Remember to exercise critical judgment about the credibility and authoritativeness of any sources and their content, selecting those that are truly in communion with the Catholic Church's teaching and the Catholic faith. The more you read, the more you will find which authors and sources are truly good. The "References and Selected Sources" list and the "Appendix: Recommended Sources About the Catholic Faith" provide you with great starting places for advancing in your faith journey and the quest for a faithful career.

Unceasing Prayer

We each have a desire for God, and He has a desire for us. The means to commune with God is prayer, including meditation. Although we already have addressed prayer at other times in this book, it is so vital to a faithful career and faith-filled life that it is worth treating again. Prayer as an isolated act of communion with God is good, and we need to take that focused time to lift our hearts and minds to God. But, as Henri Nouwen in *The Only Necessary Thing* explains, St. Paul spoke about prayer in 1 Thessalonians (5:17) radically differently than we do, even today as in his time. St. Paul "does not speak about prayer as a part of life, but as all of life" (p. 107). *When all we think, feel, and do are themselves acts of prayer done in the presence of God for God, we pray unceasingly.* In times and circumstances that are good, bad, and in between, such unceasing prayer is very good and what is essential in our relationship with God along with focused prayer time.

Thomas Merton, in his conference, "Prayer and Meditation on the Meaning of Life," explains this topic so well and ties it to work:

> God reveals himself in history, and God reveals himself to us in our life.... He reveals himself to me and to you individually as our creator and as our savior and as our father. And what we have to do, then, is we have to learn to see and to interpret the way our life goes in such a way that we can tell God's intervention in our life...and giving meaning to certain things. We can tell the difference between the things that we do that have a meaning in relation to our search for God and the things that have no meaning. You can't tell the difference, if you don't meditate on life.... Certainly at work. One of the things a person has to do is to understand the meaning of the things that happen at work.... One of the things that indicates my meaning, the meaning in my life is how I work. If I'm working in a certain way and so forth, it may show something I need to know about my life—how I'm going

along, how I'm developing, the relations with the people I work with.
There may be something in there that says something about my life.

(track 5)

All these thoughts, feelings, and behaviors intertwine, and our presentation of them to God *while we think, feel, and act* is joyful, prayerful
affirmation about God's primacy in our lives and that we hide nothing
from Him. (We could not hide anything if we wanted to.) To engage in
unceasing prayer takes discipline, perseverance, humility, faith, hope,
and charity. In fact, ample scholarship shows great benefits from pausing in one's work when practical to briefly reflect and recharge, which is
perfect for prayer.

There is no hiding from God, who loves us deeply. Unceasing prayer
involves always tossing away our egos, making ourselves vulnerable, and
always being open to conversion to become new, better people by acqui-
escing to our faults and failings then amending our lives accordingly.
That vulnerability also allows us to view our merits and triumphs not as
reflections on ourselves but, rather, evidence for the glory of God working through us. As Thomas Merton explained in *Life and Holiness*, "We
can only become saints by facing ourselves, by assuming full responsibility for our lives just as they are, with all their handicaps and limitations,
and submitting ourselves to the purifying and transforming action of the
Savior" (p. 60). In this way we properly order the good we do toward
God and not selfishly attribute to ourselves. We, then, model the virtues
that are so central to good Catholic living—to being Good people, Good
workers in the Lord's vineyard.

Other Lay Catholics

We Catholics are all in this life together—we share such a deep and ex-
pansive religious faith and tradition divinely established by Jesus Christ.
Indeed, as Catholics who have received the graces of the sacrament of
Confirmation, we are especially expected to continue to learn, apply, and
evangelize the faith with "a good zeal which separates from evil and leads
to God and everlasting life" (St. Benedict, *Rule* 72:2). So why not help
each other? And why not help those on the path to Confirmation or those
curious about Catholicism or interested in becoming Catholic? Actually,
many Catholics do help others, and such helpfulness is very apparent
through the work done and activities held in individual parishes and di-
oceses. Certainly, there are Catholic organizations operating everywhere
in the world, and they also can use the help we Catholics can give them.

Because you may be embarking on your own quest to be a Catholic
with a faithful career and faith-filled life, remember to investigate what
is already available locally. Beginning with your parish's pastor, there
will be an organizational scheme for all aspects of the parish's operation,

including faith formation. Examples of parish-based efforts include retreats; study groups focused on one or more books; lectures, seminars, and workshops; prayer groups; parish-based functional teams; and others based on parishioners' needs and available resources. Sometimes resources and programs will be jointly sponsored by two or more parishes, which is good because it spreads wide the network of Catholics in a geographic area.

Whether any activities or programs, including liturgical celebrations, are shared across parishes, the purpose is singular: To help people strengthen their relationships with God and grow in the Catholic faith. That purpose extends beyond baptized and confirmed Catholics to people who are curious about the faith and the Church, whether or not they want to become Catholic. Programs such as RCIA are instrumental in instructing people, Catholics and non-Catholics alike, in matters of the faith and the Church. In tune with the first spiritual spark for this chapter, Catholics helping other Catholics is a dynamic way to grow in the faith and strengthen your relationship with God. There will be people like you wanting to have faithful careers and better faith-filled lives. Remember, too, that if you find anyone who is in a similar quest as you for a faithful career, invite them to join you.

Conclusion

So, where may we find help? We are surrounded by good, authoritative sources to help us have faith-filled lives and faithful careers. We must choose wisely, trusting in God in our choices. We can think of these sources as guides, much like St. Philip was to the Ethiopian eunuch in Acts of the Apostles (8:26–40). The Ethiopian was reading the book of Isaiah and St. Philip, moved by the Holy Spirit, was told to seek him out and help him. St. Philip asked, "'Do you understand what you are reading?'" The eunuch answered, "'How can I, unless someone instructs me?'" Through St. Philip's instruction, the eunuch learned, believed, was baptized, and went on living according to and evangelizing about the good news of Jesus Christ.

Also consider Jesus and the Apostles. They were in the consummate teacher-pupil relationship, Master to apprentices. Like any small group of people who gather to engage in a subject matter because of their deep personal and mutual interest, deep learning can result because of the interpersonal interaction that occurs at the cognitive, affective, and behavioral levels. The Apostles were a kind of class who learned well and deeply from Christ, then, as Jesus instructed them, they taught others plus ordained and installed leaders of the Church to establish and grow the faith and the Church simultaneously that has, in turn, lasted nearly two millennia—and "the gates of the netherworld shall not prevail against it" (Matthew 16:18). The great volume of discourse produced over the ages about the faith attests to its profundity and utility in our lives, and we must use any of it that we can to help us grow in the Catholic faith.

From our local parishes to the internet to publications to fellow Catholics we know, we have access to the credible, authoritative sources that we need to learn about, apply, and share the faith. We can use them alone or with others. Making sure any source is good is paramount, as there are enough poor sources about the Catholic faith and the Catholic Church that subvert the truth with faulty arguments and analysis (at best) and risk promoting heresy and causing people to reject the faith and the Church (at worst). Through good, credible teaching from individual sources, such as books, articles, websites, and others, we have learned guides about the Catholic faith at our fingertips. Through good, credible teaching during the sacrament of Reconciliation, lectures, workshops, webinars, and others, we have the added benefit of learned guides about the Catholic faith in person with us, like Jesus was to the Apostles and the disciples as well as how St. Philip was to the Ethiopian. Knowing now where to find good, authoritative help is liberating because there are more-than-ample places to learn and grow in the Catholic faith that will, in turn, result in faithful careers and lives.

Questions for Meditation

- How do you see yourself now in the context of the second spiritual spark for this chapter? What would be your next steps to making a faithful career through the content of this chapter?
- Given how you have thought, felt, and done in your life as a Catholic, how would you now convincingly argue to someone (even yourself) that becoming a more-engaged Catholic? What does your result mean for you to have a faithful career?
- Are there any learning opportunities in your own Catholic parish or diocese that have piqued your interest? Which ones might you want to join as a participant? Or, are there ones in which you would like to be a leader? Based on what you learn about them, discern which one is right for you and join!

Suggested Activities for Application

- Take a look at Pope St. John Paul II's encyclical, *Christifideles Laici*, which is available on the Vatican's website. Identify some concepts or principles that stand out to you and think about why they do. Then consider what you can do to apply them in your life, especially at work.
- Obtain one or more books on Catholicism and work, titles for which are included in this book's references list. Find important points that inspire you to revise your view of why work is important and how you can have a better faithful career through which to give God glory.

- Get a copy of a book about the lives of the saints of the Catholic Church and read the biographies of as many as you wish. Perhaps begin with the saint(s) for your given name, or saints that are patrons for particular lines of work (e.g. the patron saints for photographers, firefighters, physicians), or saints that you find especially interesting or have wondered about, or all of these options. You also may like to look for and read about people who were not ordained/consecrated religious and are canonized saints or in the process toward possible canonization such as St. Juan Diego, St. Gianna Molla, St. Thomas More, Blessed Carlo Acutis, Blessed Anna Kolesárová, Blessed Ivan Merz, and Venerable Antonietta Meo. See how very ordinary their lives were and, particularly, how they overcame struggles in their lives to draw so much closer to God. Think about the ordinariness of your life and how the lives of these holy people can help you draw closer to God yourself through surrender and conversion.

6   When Do We Take the Next Steps?

Brothers and sisters: Whoever sows sparingly will also reap sparingly, and whoever sows bountifully will also reap bountifully. Each must do as already determined, without sadness or compulsion, for God loves a cheerful giver. Moreover, God is able to make every grace abundant for you, so that in all things, always having all you need, you may have an abundance for every good work.

(2 Corinthians 9:6–8)

I urge you therefore, brothers, by the mercies of God, to offer your bodies as a living sacrifice, holy and pleasing to God, your spiritual worship. Do not conform yourselves to this age but be transformed by the renewal of your mind, that you may discern what is the will of God, what is good and pleasing and perfect.

(Romans 12:1–2)

I think back to all the first days on the job that I have had in my career, even going back to my paper route. How stressful they were in their own ways just because they were beginnings. I would not have a job, if I did not take the steps to obtain it. I then had to take the next step to report to work the first day. On that day I started working with people I did not know and had so much to learn and so much that was new to care about. Note, however, that the stressfulness of that first day was not necessarily bad. Good stress is energizing, heightens awareness, focuses thinking, reveals possibilities, and opens pathways to good work. The more I continued in my jobs, the more next steps I took, even with missteps too at times. The more I worked in my jobs, the more value I could add and did add. My strong, positive work ethic kept me going, even in the face of trials as well as triumphs. As I reflect on that work ethic, I can see the Catholicity in it that has served me well. And I have needed a special boost through the Catholic faith from time to time.

Life involves a series of next steps that we take, especially with the guidance of the Holy Spirit about God's will, to advance from those we take on our journey to eternity with God. Look again and reflect on the two scriptural sparks that begin this chapter. In many ways, these excerpts summarize the content and the purpose for this book. We reap what we sow, and as humble workers in the Lord's vineyard using our God-given wherewithal, we should reap abundantly from what we sow abundantly. Pope Francis, in *Gaudete et Exsultate*, advises us about God's call to us: "The important thing is that each believer discern his or her own path, that they bring out the very best of themselves, the most personal gifts that God has placed in their hearts" (§11).

In doing our work, building our careers, and living our lives, we must keep our hearts and minds on God and His will, not on the fancies of the world. Archbishop Charles Chaput explains this point well:

> Catholics can live quite peacefully with the separation of Church and state, so long as the arrangement translates into real religious freedom. But we can never accept a separation of our religious faith and moral convictions from our public ministries or our political engagement. It's impossible. And even *trying* is evil because it forces us to live two different lives, worshiping God at home and in our churches; and worshiping the latest version of Caesar everywhere else. That turns our private convictions into lies we tell ourselves and each other.... *Religious faith sincerely believed and humbly lived serves human dignity. It fosters virtue, not conflict. Therefore it can be vital in building a humane society.*
>
> (paras. 5–6; italics in original)

What is at stake here is what we are to be and to do as Catholics and caretakers of God's creation. At the end of the Mass, we are given the charge to "Glorify the Lord by your life." In other words, we are to directly apply Jesus' teachings in every aspect of our lives and for the world. To reinforce this pivotal principle, Pope Pius XII stated in 1946,

> The moral order and God's commandments have a force equally in all fields of human activity. As far as the fields stretch, so far extends the mission of the Church, and also her teachings, warnings, and the counsel of the priest to the faithful confined to his care....The Catholic Church will never allow herself to be shut up within the four walls of the temple. The separation between religion and life, between the Church and the world is contrary to the Christian and Catholic idea.
>
> (qtd. in & trans. by Cranny, 1952, p. xvii)

It is important to remember that, even though we probably do not think about it, our ordinary daily lives are loaded with innumerable opportunities of simplicity that offer essential, even mundane acts and sacrifices that bring us closer to God, even the basic matter of getting along well with other people (particularly those with whom we are not fond of). Importantly, the ordinary and mundane things of life far exceed the very infrequent grandiose things. In this way, then, simplicity is the profound key to working well in God's vineyard, which is consistent with the teachings of St. Benedict in his *Rule*, what St. Thérèse of Lisieux teaches us in her "little way," and is reflected in so many other good examples from people who are canonized saints *and* who are not but known dearly to us as good examples.

The richness of the Catholic faith, as this book has only meekly introduced, provides us with so much to guide our journey in holiness to God and to do so in our work and careers. Pope Francis in *Fratelli Tutti* explains,

> God encourages us to develop the talents he gave us, and he has made our universe one of immense potential. In God's plan, each individual is called to promote his or her own development, and this includes finding the best economic and technological means of multiplying goods and increasing wealth. Business abilities, which are a gift from God, should always be clearly directed to the development of others and to eliminating poverty, especially through the creation of diversified work opportunities.
>
> (§123)

We must choose to engage in the Catholic faith and engage in it well always, from home, to work, to anywhere. Being more knowledgeable about the Catholic faith (at least with this book as a start), embracing it and its teachings genuinely as means for living in Christ, and then acting well on them little by little out of love—the love of Christ—in all things always are truly instrumental as a Catholic with a faithful career and faith-filled life.

The dynamic intersection of prayer, work, and study, as St. Benedict explained in his *Rule* more than 1,400 years ago, is so important to living holy lives in communion with God through the Catholic faith. Because our souls yearn for God and His graces, we learn and evangelize through our lives—particularly in our thoughts, attitudes, and behaviors—to give Him glory in all that we are and do. "Who among you is wise and understanding? Let him show his works by a good life in the humility that comes from wisdom" (James 3:13). A faithful career amid a faith-filled life that reflects right priorities toward God is ours to have and enjoy, as workers in the Lord's vineyard. With this simplest and final chapter of this book, Psalm 90 (14–17) offers an inspiring perspective for our lives and careers from which we can begin each day:

> 14 Fill us at daybreak with your mercy,
>   that all our days we may sing for joy.
> 15 Make us glad as many days as you humbled us,
>   for as many years as we have seen trouble.

16 Show your deeds to your servants,
   your glory to their children.
17 May the favor of the Lord our God be ours.
   Prosper the work of our hands!
   Prosper the work of our hands!

Conclusion

So, when do we take the next steps to integrate the Catholic faith and work? The simple answer is *now!* "Every journey begins with the first step," as the old saying goes. To not take the first step is to not embark on the journey. We take any journey because we need the gifts from it. In these statements, a destination is only implied because the journey is more valuable than the end point, which is the culminating reward for a successful journey. The gifts from the journey itself keep us focused on continuing the quest to its end because all of it is worthwhile, even if that means taking a side trip from time to time—eventually we get back on track and have received other gifts from that side trip too. (Even a failed journey has gifts.) On any journey, roadblocks, potholes, breakdowns, and detours happen without much or any forewarning, and they are surmountable with some extra effort so that we can regain our course.

If those roadblocks, potholes, breakdowns, and detours cause us to reconsider the journey and quit to pursue some other trek, it is best to first take some time to discern that option and whether it is truly good to embark on a different quest. In other words, sleep on it—like Psalm 127 (2) says, "God gives to his beloved in sleep." Sometimes in life we need to do that, especially in our jobs and for our careers. For us Catholics, our faith journey can be similar, but the difference is Christ and all the teachings of the Catholic Church that support us in our Catholic faith so that, by living holy lives and having faithful careers, we can reach the final destination of eternity with God, Jesus Christ, the Holy Spirit, and all the saints. Let these words from Jesus Christ inspire you daily for your faithful career:

Be not afraid.
Go and make disciples of all nations.
I am with you always, until the end of the age.
Peace be with you.

Questions for Meditation

- What will be your next step to having a faithful career? How will you integrate the Catholic faith into your life and the lives of your loved ones?
- How has the Catholic Church empowered people to improve themselves individually and participate well in civic society? What are the

grave dangers of forsaking the Catholic faith yourself and for the world?

- How will you continue to learn, apply, and share the Catholic faith well at work? What factors do you anticipate would influence you, and how can you use them reasonably, possibly even improving them for the benefit of others and the organization by blending effectively religion/spirituality in the workplace? What questions do you have left to answer?

Suggested Activities for Application

- Using the Appendix to this book, begin using the sources listed there one at a time to advance your learning about the Catholic faith and the Catholic Church at your own pace. Keep notes about what you read and what you learn from what you read. Pose questions or make comments about which you would like to explore separately, perhaps by talking with a priest, nun, brother, or sister in the Catholic orders of religious, or perhaps through the other activities given here.

- If you have not taken a Bible study course of some kind, it is time you did. An excellent one in book form is Tim Gray and Jeff Cavins' book, *Walking with God: A Journey Through the Bible* (revised edition, Ascension Press, 2018) and their *Bible Timeline*. The book with the timeline traces salvation history from Genesis to Revelation, explaining how the interconnectedness of all the books of the Bible leads to Jesus as the Christ, His establishing the Catholic Church, and the ultimate salvation when He comes again. Cavins' DVD set, *The Great Adventure: The Bible Timeline* (Ascension Press), is a great companion to the book's content.

- Enroll in a formal program about the Catholic faith to learn more deeply about and apply more broadly matters of the faith in all aspects of your life. Such programs include an RCIA (Rite of Christian Initiation of Adults) program held at your or another parish, religious formation programs in your diocese, the series of programs offered through Word on Fire, degree or certificate programs offered through Catholic institutions of higher education, or the educational resources offered online through the Knights of Columbus' Catholic Information Service (CIS).

Prayer for Working Well for God in His Vineyard

Dear God,

I believe You led me to where I am today—my place, roles, and station in this life—so that I may fulfill Your Holy Will. I thank You for the talents You've given me, and I thank the Holy Spirit for the charisms given to me. I need Your help in discerning my charisms and using them and my talents excellently to give You glory in everything I think, say, and do. In the name of Jesus Christ, I humbly ask You—Father, Son, and Holy Spirit—together with the Blessed Mother, my patron saints, and my guardian angel, to drive away all evil spirits from me and use me as You see fit as Your instrument of goodness, wisdom, peace, mercy, and love. Amen.

~ Peter M. Smudde

References and Selected Sources

The following list of sources includes both those used in this book and those you may use to extend your learning beyond this book. The titles of the sources are sufficiently descriptive to indicate their content, so you may choose ones that most interest you at the times you need them.

À Kempis, T. (2003). *The imitation of Christ.* Mineola, MN: Dover Thrift Editions. (Originally published 1940 from author's work published c. 1418–1427).

Abela, A. V., & Capizzi, J. E. (Eds.) (2014). *A catechism for business: Tough ethical questions and insights from Catholic teaching.* Washington, DC: Catholic University of America Press.

Aburdene, P. (2007). *Megatrends 2010: The rise of conscious capitalism.* Charlottesville, VA: Hampton Roads Publishing.

Akin, J. (n.d.). *Dogma, doctrine, and theology: What are they?* Retrieved from http://jimmyakin.com/dogma-doctrine-and-theology-what-are-they

Annuario Pontificio 2019 (2019). Dicastero per il Servizio Dello Sviluppo Umano Integrale [Dicastery for Promoting Pntegral Human Development]. Retrieved from http://www.vatican.va/roman_curia/sviluppo-umano-integrale/documents/rc_sviluppo-umano-integrale_20170509_note-storiche_it.html [English translation generated online by Google]

Banks, R. J. (Ed.) (1999). *Faith goes to work: Reflection from the marketplace.* Eugene, OR: Wipf and Stock Publishers.

Barron, R. (2011). *Catholicism: A journey to the heart of the faith.* New York: Image Books. [Based on his documentary video series of the same title]

Barron, R. (2019). *Letter to a suffering church: A bishop speaks on the sexual abuse crisis.* Park Ridge, IL: Word on Fire.

Bunge, G. (2012). *Despondency: The spiritual teaching of Evagrius Ponticus on acedia.* Yonkers, NY: St. Vladimir's Seminary Press.

Carpenter, D. (2015, February 10). Indifference to the dignity of work. *Catholic Stand.* Retrieved from https://www.catholicstand.com/indifference-dignity-work/

Carpenter, D. (2015, April 8). A work week theology. *Catholic Stand.* Retrieved from https://www.catholicstand.com/a-work-week-theology/

Carpenter, D. (2016, January 16). Answering the call to work. *Catholic Stand.* Retrieved from https://www.catholicstand.com/a-calling-to-work/

Carpenter, D. (2016, March 16). Five things every Catholic business person must know. *Catholic Stand.* Retrieved from https://www.catholicstand.com/5-things-that-every-catholic-businessperson-must-know/

Carrascoso, A. C. (2014). A framework for a Catholic stakeholder core. *Journal of Management, Spirituality, and Religion, 11*(4), 307–330. Retrieved from http://dx.doi.org/10.1080/14766086.2014.913496

Catechism of the Catholic Church, 2nd edition (1997). Washington, DC: United States Catholic Conference.

Catholic News Agency (2020, May 19). *Labor Department issues new religious freedom guidelines.* Retrieved from https://www.catholicnewsagency.com/news/labor-department-issues-new-religious-freedom-guidelines-19560

Chaput, C. J. (2012, September 15). *"We have no king but Caesar": Some thoughts on Catholic faith and public life.* Retrieved from https://catholicphilly.com/2012/09/homilies-speeches/we-have-no-king-but-caesar-some-thoughts-on-catholic-faith-and-public-life/

Compendium: Catechism of the Catholic Church (2006). Washington, DC: United States Conference of Catholic Bishops Publishing.

Corbitt, S. (2018). *Fulfilled: Uncovering the Biblical foundations of Catholicism.* West Chester, PA: Ascension Press

Cosden, D. (2004). *A theology of work: Work and the new creation.* Eugene, OR: Wipf & Stock Publishers.

Cranny, T. (1952). *The moral obligation of voting.* Washington, DC: Catholic University of America Press. [Doctoral dissertation] Retrieved from https://www.radioregina.info/site/bibliotheque/Morale/P%E8re%20Cranny%20S.A.%20-%20The%20Moral%20Obligation%20of%20Voting.pdf

Dicastery for Promoting Integral Human Development (2018). *Vocation of the business leader: A reflection* (5th ed.). St. Thomas, MN: John A. Ryan Institute for Catholic Social Thought of the Center for Catholic Studies at the University of St. Thomas. Retrieved from https://www.stthomas.edu/media/catholicstudies/center/ryan/publications/publicationpdfs/vocationofthebusinessleaderpdf/FinalTextTheVocationoftheBusinessLeader.pdf

Dicastery for Promoting Integral Human Development (n.d.). *The Dicastery.* Retrieved from http://www.humandevelopment.va/en/il-dicastero.html

Dik, B. J., & Duffy, R. D. (2012). *Make your job a calling: How the psychology of vocation can change your life at work.* West Conshohocken, PA: Templeton Press.

Dolan, T. M. (2009). *Doers of the word: Putting your faith in practice.* Huntington, IN: Our Sunday Visitor.

Dorr, D. (2006). *Faith at work: A spirituality of leadership.* Collegeville, MN: Liturgical Press.

Gallagher, T. M. (2009). *Discerning the will of God: An Ignatian guide to Christian decision making.* New York: Crossroad Publishing Company.

Guardini, R. (n.d.). *The art of praying: The principles and methods of Christian prayer.* Manchester, NH: Sophia Institute Press. (Original work published 1985).

Hahn, S. (2007). *Reasons to believe: How to understand, explain, and defend the Catholic faith.* London, UK: Darton, Longman & Todd.

Hahnenberg, E. P. (2007). *A concise guide to the documents of Vatican II.* Cincinnati, OH: St. Anthony Messenger Press.

Hain, R. (2011). *The Catholic briefcase: Tools for integrating faith and work.* Liguori, MO: Liguori Publications.

Hain, R. (2016, June 23). Six ways to avoid being a "stealth" Catholic. *The Integrated Catholic Life*. Retrieved from http://www.integratedcatholiclife. org/2016/06/randy-hain-six-ways-to-avoid-being-a-stealth-catholic/

Hain, R. (2017, September 21). Practical lessons for integrating faith and work. *Integrated Catholic Life*. Retrieved from http://www.integratedcatholiclife. org/2017/09/randy-hain-practical-lessons-for-integrating-faith-and-work-2/

Hitchcock, J. (2012). *Chesterton*. San Francisco, CA: Ignatius Press.

Horn, T. (2017). *Why we're Catholic: Our reasons for faith, hope, and love*. El Cajon, CA: Catholic Answers Press.

Ivereigh, A., & Lopez, K. J. (2015). *How to defend the faith without raising our voice: Civil responses to Catholic hot-button issues*. Huntington, IN: Our Sunday Visitor.

Jacobs, S. (2016, February 22). What good is it to gain the whole world if you lose your soul?–Saying yes to God's will. *Catholic Stand*. Retrieved from https://www. catholicstand.com/good-gain-whole-world-lose-soul-saying-yes-gods-will/

Jacobs, S. (2016, April 14). How do we know God's will? Careers and God's call. *Catholic Stand*. Retrieved from https://www.catholicstand.com/ know-gods-will-careers-gods-call/

Kaczor, C. (2012). *The seven big myths about the Catholic Church: Distinguishing fact from fiction about Catholicism*. San Francisco, CA: Ignatius Press.

Kelly, M. (2010). *Rediscover Catholicism: A spiritual guide to living with passion and purpose*. North Palm Beach, FL: Beacon Publishing.

Kelly, M. (2014). *Faith at work and the holy moment* [audio CD]. North Palm Beach, FL: Beacon Publishing.

Kelly, M. (2017). *Perfectly yourself: Discovering God's dream for you* (new & revised ed.). North Palm Beach, FL: Beacon.

Kelly, M. (2018). *The biggest lie in the history of Christianity*. North Palm Beach, FL: Eucalyptus Media Group.

Kniaz, P. (2017, September 18). Idleness and work in the letter to the Thessalonians. *Catholic Stand*. Retrieved from https://www.catholicstand.com/ idleness-work-letter-thessalonians/

Kreeft, P. J., & Tacelli, R. K. (2009). *Handbook of Catholic apologetics: Reasoned answers to questions of faith*. San Francisco, CA: Ignatius Press.

Machado, J. (2016, April 12). Motivated by love: Working despite criticism. *Catholic Stand*. Retrieved from https://www.catholicstand.com/ motivated-by-love-working-despite-criticism/

Marketdata Enterprises Inc. (2019, October 17). *$11 billion self-improvement market is growing—by John LaRosa*. Retrieved from https://www.marketdataenterprises. com/11-billion-self-improvement-market-is-growing-by-john-larosa/

Martin, J., & Langford, J. (Eds.) (2002). *Professions of faith: Living and working as a Catholic*. Franklin, MI: Sheed & Ward.

Merton, T. (1963). *Life and holiness*. New York: Herder and Herder.

Merton, T. (2012). Prayer and meditation on the meaning of life. In *Thomas Merton on Contemplation* [audio CD]. Rockville, MD: Now You Know Media. (Recorded January 28, 1964).

Mitroff, I. I., & Denton, E. A. (1999). *A spiritual audit of corporate America: A hard look at spirituality, religion, and values in the workplace*. San Francisco, CA: Jossey-Bass.

Naughton, M. (2019). *Getting work right: Labor and leisure in a fragmented world.* Steubenville, OH: Emmaus Road Publishing.

Nault, J. C. (2013). *The noonday devil: Acedia, the unnamed evil of our times.* San Francisco, CA: Ignatius Press.

Nolan, J. L. (2006). *Doing the right thing at work: A Catholic's guide to faith, business, and ethics.* Cincinnati, OH: St. Anthony Messenger Press.

Norris, K. (2008). *Acedia and me: A marriage, monks, and a writer's life.* New York: Riverhead Books.

Novak, M. (1996). *Business as a calling: Work and the examined life.* New York: The Free Press.

Oldroyd-Bolt, D. (2019, April 24). Pilgrimage is good for employees, study concludes. *Catholic Herald.* Retrieved from https://catholicherald.co.uk/news/2019/04/24/pilgrimage-is-good-for-employees-study-concludes/

Pew Research Center. (2018, November 20). *Where Americans find meaning in life: Economic, religious and political divides shape where Americans find meaning – but family, career and friendship emerge as common themes.* Washington, DC: Author. Retrieved from https://www.pewforum.org/2018/11/20/where-americans-find-meaning-in-life/

Pfeffer, J. (2010). Business and the spirit: Management practices that sustain values. In R. A. Giacalone & C. L. Jurkiewicz (Eds.), *Handbook of workplace spirituality and organizational performance* (2nd ed., pp. 27–43). Armonk, NY: M.E. Sharpe Inc.

Philippe, J. (2008). *Time for God.* New Rochelle, NY: Scepter.

Pierce, G. F. A. (Ed.) (1991). *Of human hands: A reader in the spirituality of work.* Minneapolis, MN: Augsburg.

Pierce, G. F. A. (2001). *Spirituality at work: 10 ways to balance your life on the job.* Chicago, IL: Loyola Press.

Pierce, G. F. A. (2004). *Finding God @ work: Practicing spirituality in your workplace.* Plainfield, NJ: RENEW International.

Pontifical Council for Justice and Peace (2005). *Compendium of the social doctrine of the church.* Washington, DC: United States Conference of Catholic Bishops.

Pontifical Council for Justice and Peace (n.d.). Retrieved from http://www.vatican.va/roman_curia/pontifical_councils/justpeace/documents/rc_pc_justpeace_pro_20011004_en.html

Pope Benedict XVI (2008). *Church fathers: From Clement of Rome to Augustine.* San Francisco, CA: Ignatius Press.

Pope Benedict XVI (2009). *Caritas in veritate (Charity in truth).* Vatican: The Holy See. Retrieved from http://w2.vatican.va/content/benedict-xvi/en/encyclicals/documents/hf_ben-xvi_enc_20090629_caritas-in-veritate.html

Pope Francis (2013). *Evangelii Gaudium (Joy of the Gospel).* Vatican: The Holy See. Retrieved from http://w2.vatican.va/content/francesco/en/apost_exhortations/documents/papa-francesco_esortazione-ap_20131124_evangelii-gaudium.html

Pope Francis (2015). *Laudato Si' (On care for our common home).* Vatican: The Holy See. Retrieved from http://w2.vatican.va/content/francesco/en/encyclicals/documents/papa-francesco_20150524_enciclica-laudato-si.html

Pope Francis (2015, October 31). *Address of his holiness Pope Francis to the Christian Union of Business Executives (UCID).* Retrieved from http://

w2.vatican.va/content/francesco/en/speeches/2015/october/documents/
papa-francesco_20151031_ucid.html

Pope Francis (2017). *Letter of the Holy Father Francis to the participants in the international conference "From* Populorum Progressio *to Laudato Si'."* Vatican: The Holy See. Retrieved from http://w2.vatican.va/content/francesco/en/
letters/2017/documents/papa-francesco_20171123_lettera-turkson-encicliche.
html

Pope Francis (2018). *Gaudete et exsultate (On the call to holiness in today's world)*. Vatican: The Holy See. Retrieved from http://www.vatican.va/content/
francesco/en/apost_exhortations/documents/papa-francesco_esortazione-
ap_20180319_gaudete-et-exsultate.html

Pope Francis (2020). *Fratelli tutti (On fraternity and social friendship)*. Vatican: The Holy See. Retrieved from http://www.vatican.va/content/francesco/en/
encyclicals/documents/papa-francesco_20201003_enciclica-fratelli-tutti.html

Pope John XXIII (1961). *Mater et magistra (On Christianity and social progress)*. Vatican: The Holy See. Retrieved from http://w2.vatican.va/content/john-xxiii/
en/encyclicals/documents/hf_j-xxiii_enc_15051961_mater.html

Pope John Paul II (1981). *Laborem exercens (On human work)*. Vatican City: The Holy See. Retrieved from http://w2.vatican.va/content/john-paul-ii/en/
encyclicals/documents/hf_jp-ii_enc_14091981_laborem-exercens.html

Pope John Paul II (1987). *Sollicitudo rei socialis (Church's concern for the social order)*. Vatican: The Holy See. Retrieved from http://w2.vatican.va/content/
john-paul-ii/en/encyclicals/documents/hf_jp-ii_enc_30121987_sollicitudo-
rei-socialis.html

Pope John Paul II (1988). *Christifideles laici (The vocation and mission of the lay faithful in the church and the world)*. Vatican City: The Holy See. Retrieved from http://w2.vatican.va/content/john-paul-ii/en/apost_exhortations/
documents/hf_jp-ii_exh_30121988_christifideles-laici.html

Pope John Paul II (1991). *Centesimus annus (On the hundredth anniversary of* Rerum Novarum). Vatican: The Holy See. Retrieved from https://w2.vatican.
va/content/john-paul-ii/en/encyclicals/documents/hf_jp-ii_enc_01051991_
centesimus-annus.html

Pope Leo XIII (1891). *Rerum novarum (On capital and labor)*. Vatican City: The Holy See. Retrieved from http://w2.vatican.va/content/leo-xiii/en/encyclicals/
documents/hf_l-xiii_enc_15051891_rerum-novarum.html

Pope Paul VI (1967). *Populorum progressio (On the development of peoples)*. Vatican: The Holy See. Retrieved from http://w2.vatican.va/content/paul-vi/en/
encyclicals/documents/hf_p-vi_enc_26031967_populorum.html

Pope Pius XI (1931). *Quadragesimo anno (On the reconstruction of the social order)*. Vatican City: The Holy See. Retrieved from http://w2.vatican.va/
content/pius-xi/en/encyclicals/documents/hf_p-xi_enc_19310515_quadragesimo-
anno.html

Ratzinger, J. (Pope Benedict XVI) (2004). *Introduction to Christianity* (Trans. J. R. Foster). San Francisco, CA: Communio Books/Ignatius Press.

Robinson, H. W. (Ed.) (2015). *Theology of work Bible commentary:* Genesis *through* Revelation (one volume ed.). Peabody, MA: Hendrickson Publishers.

Roccas, N. M. (2017). *Time and despondency: Regaining the present in faith and life*. Chesterton, IN: Ancient Faith Publishing.

Rock, M. (2015). *St. Benedict's guide to improving your work life: Workplace as worthplace*. New London, CT: Twenty Third Publications.

Royal, R. (2017, September 4). The recent popes on work and workers. *The Catholic Thing*. Retrieved from https://www.thecatholicthing.org/2017/09/04/the-recent-popes-on-work-and-workers/

Saint Augustine (1998). *Confessions*. New York: Oxford University Press. (Original written 396–399).

Saint Benedict (1982). *The rule of St. Benedict in English* (T. Fry, editor). Collegeville, MN: Liturgical Press. (Originally written c. 530).

Saint Faustina Kowalska (2002). *Diary: Divine mercy in my soul*. Stockbridge, MA: Marians of the Immaculate Conception.

Saint Ignatius of Antioch (105). *The epistle of Ignatius to the Smyrnaeans*. Retrieved from https://www.newadvent.org/fathers/0109.htm

Salza, J. (2005). *The Biblical basis for the Catholic faith*. Huntington, IN: Our Sunday Visitor.

Schlag, M., & Melé, D. (2019). *A Catholic spirituality for business: The logic of gift*. Washington, DC: The Catholic University of America Press.

Scupoli, L. (2013). *The spiritual combat*. London, UK: Catholic Way Publishing. (Originally published in 1945 from author's work published c. 1589 and thereafter).

Second Vatican Council (Vatican II) (1963). *Sacrosanctum concilium (Constitution on the sacred liturgy)*. Vatican: The Holy See. Retrieved from https://www.vatican.va/archive/hist_councils/ii_vatican_council/documents/vat-ii_const_19631204_sacrosanctum-concilium_en.html

Second Vatican Council (Vatican II) (1964). *Lumen gentium (Dogmatic constitution on the church)*. Vatican City: The Holy See. Retrieved from http://www.vatican.va/archive/hist_councils/ii_vatican_council/documents/vat-ii_const_19641121_lumen-gentium_en.html

Second Vatican Council (Vatican II) (1965a). *Gaudium et spes (Pastoral constitution on the church in the modern world)*. Vatican: The Holy See. Retrieved from http://www.vatican.va/archive/hist_councils/ii_vatican_council/documents/vat-ii_const_19651207_gaudium-et-spes_en.html

Second Vatican Council (Vatican II) (1965b). *Apostolicam actuositatem (On the apostolate of the laity)*. Vatican City: The Holy See. Retrieved from http://www.vatican.va/archive/hist_councils/ii_vatican_council/documents/vat-ii_decree_19651118_apostolicam-actuositatem_en.html

Shaw, R. (2013). *Catholic laity in the mission of the church: Living your personal vocation* (new expanded ed.). Langley City, British Columbia, Canada: Chartwell Press.

Skrabec Jr., Q. R. (2003). *St. Benedict's rule for business success*. West Lafayette, IN: Purdue University Press.

Snell, R. J. (2015). *Acedia and its discontents: Metaphysical boredom in an empire of desire*. Kettering, OH: Angelico Press.

Society of Human Resource Management (2008). *Religion and corporate culture: Accommodating religious diversity in the workplace*. Alexandria, VA: Author. Retrieved from https://www.shrm.org/hr-today/trends-and-forecasting/research-and-surveys/documents/08-0625religionsr_updtfinal.pdf

Socks, P. (2015, December 18). Labor: We work the whole day through. *Catholic Stand.* Retrieved from https://www.catholicstand.com/laborwe-work-the-whole-day-through/

Sri, E. (2011). *A biblical walk through the Mass: Understanding what we say and do in the liturgy.* West Chester, PA: Ascension Press.

U. S. Department of Labor (2020, May 15). *U.S. Department of Labor advances protection for religious liberty.* Retrieved from https://www.dol.gov/newsroom/releases/dol/dol20200515

Vest, N. (1997). *Friend of the soul: A Benedictine spirituality of work.* Cambridge, MA: Cowley Publications.

Ward, B. (2003). *The desert fathers: Sayings of the early Christian monks.* New York: Penguin Books.

Weber, C. (2014, February 3). Don't underestimate your Catholic work ethic. *Catholic Stand.* Retrieved from https://www.catholicstand.com/dont-underestimate-catholic-work-ethic/

Weber, C. (2015, May 20). Five steps to maximize the value of your work. *Catholic Stand.* Retrieved from https://www.catholicstand.com/five-steps-to-maximize-the-value-of-your-work/

Weddell, S. A. (1998). *The Catholic spiritual gifts inventory* (3rd ed.). Colorado Springs, CO: The Siena Institute Press.

Weddell, S. A. (2012). *Forming intentional disciples: The path to knowing and following Jesus.* Huntington, IN: Our Sunday Visitor.

Appendix

Recommended Sources About the Catholic Faith

Books (Alphabetized by Author after the First Entry)

Catechism of the Catholic Church (2nd edition)
Why Believe? (2 volumes) by Augustine Institute
Catholicism by Bishop Robert Barron
Letter to a Suffering Church, by Bishop Robert Barron
Bible Basics for Catholics by John Bergsma
Living the Catholic Life by Archbishop Charles Chaput
Fulfilled by Sonja Corbitt
Doers of the Word by Cardinal Timothy Dolan
Catholic Customs & Traditions: A Popular Guide by Greg Dues
Why I Love Being Catholic by The Dynamic Catholic Institute
Believing in Jesus by Leonard Foley
Walking with God by Tim Gray and Jeff Cavins
Reasons to Believe by Scott Hahn
Why We're Catholic by Trent Horn
How to Defend the Faith Without Raising Your Voice by Austen Ivereigh &
    Kathryn Jean Lopez
The Seven Myths of the Catholic Church by Christopher Kaczor
Rediscover Catholicism by Matthew Kelly
Four Signs of a Dynamic Catholic by Matthew Kelly
The Biggest Lie in the History of Christianity by Matthew Kelly
Introduction to Christianity by Cardinal Joseph Ratzinger
The Biblical Basis for the Catholic Church by John Salza
Love Unveiled by Edward Sri
The Catholic Church Through the Ages (2nd edition) by John Vidmar, OP
The Courage to be Catholic by George Weigel
The Truth of Catholicism by George Weigel

Online and Digital Resources (some also offer mobile phone apps)

The Vatican (http://w2.vatican.va/content/vatican/en.html)
United States Council of Catholic Bishops (http://www.usccb.org/)
Catholic Answers (https://www.catholic.com/)

Catholic Apostolate Center (https://www.catholicapostolatecenter.org/)

Catholic Education Resource Center (https://www.catholiceducation.org/en/)

Catholic Encyclopedia (http://www.newadvent.org/cathen/)

Dynamic Catholic (https://dynamiccatholic.com/)

Formed (https://formed.org/)

National Black Catholic Congress (https://www.nbccongress.org/)

Word on Fire (https://www.wordonfire.org/)

Vatican News (https://www.vaticannews.va/en.html)

Catholic News Agency (https://www.catholicnewsagency.com)

Also look for your state's Catholic Conference

Index

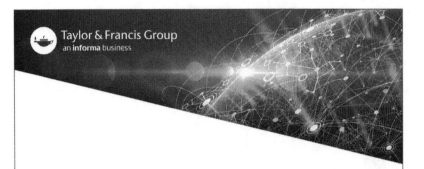